JESUS
IN IRAN

EUGENE BACH

Jesus in Iran

By Eugene Bach
Author of the Underground Church

Published by
Back to Jerusalem
277 Lower Airport Road
Lumberton, MS 39455
www.backtojerusalem.com

ISBN: 978-0-692-50099-6
eBook ISBN: 978-0-692-50100-6

Printed in the United States of America
© 2015 by Back to Jerusalem, Inc.

Library of Congress Cataloging-in-Publication Data (Pending)

CONTENTS

INTRODUCTION

In the winter of 2014, I found myself standing at a place that is often referred to as Revolution Square in Tehran, the capital city of Iran. I was waiting on a ride from an Iranian underground house church coordinator. Fragrant aromas from the many food vendors at every street corner were rising into the cold evening air. Traffic was congested; vehicles were bumper-to-bumper around the boarded-up center of city square. Old box-shaped cars that looked like throwbacks to Soviet-era vehicles filled the streets in Tehran.

In the distance, I could hear the faint sound of the call to prayer, but it didn't seem like anyone was paying attention. No one stopped. No one prayed.

It was a Thursday evening, which is considered the beginning of the weekend for Iranians, so there was a festive bustle in the air. Although the people weren't heeding the call to prayer, reminders that Islam is the main religion in Iran are never far away. The Iranian flag can be seen in most shops in bustling Tehran. It is still the same red, white, and green flag that was adopted in 1980, red symbolizing martyrdom and green symbolizing Islam. In the middle of the flag is a white band with a shape that looks like a tulip to most people who are not familiar with Arabic writing, but it's actually the stylized symbol for Allah and the phrase *"La ilaha illa Allah,"* meaning "none is worthy of worship but Allah." Along the inner edges of the green and red bands is the phrase *"Allah Akbar"* or "God is Great," which are usually the last words of Islamic fighters. That phrase is repeated twenty-two times on the Iranian flag. The city of Tehran has many faces. One side of Tehran is modern, progressive, and inclusive while the other side is dark, religious, and intolerant. The face of intolerance is ever present in the large posters of the Supreme Leaders Ruhollah Khomeini (who passed away in 1989) and Sayyed Ali Khamenei. These imposing posters are plastered all over the city and are constant reminders of the evil prevalent in Iran. To the Western world, they are images that recall the US embassy riot that took place more than thirty years ago. The images are a constant reminder that the Iranian government wants the Zionist Jews to be removed from the face of the earth and that Christian missionaries are not welcome.

I spent many months in the 1990s in the US military patrolling the waters west of the border of Iran in the Persian Gulf. At that time, the Iranian military was a threat that was mostly contained by Iraq.

Today, however, Iran has become unbridled and presents a clear and present danger to the rest of the world. Their nuclear program worries the neighboring Sunni countries as well as Israel. Their wealth of oil reserves provides one of the best resources for military funding of any other nation in the region. In terms of the size and strength of their military, Iran is second only to Israel.

I have not come to Iran to evaluate their threat to the rest of the world. Instead, I travel to Iran in search of platforms for Chinese missionaries. I write this book from the perspective of a Back to Jerusalem worker from China, not as an expert on Iran. I have only been working in Iran for a couple of years and am in no way qualified to debate Iranian statistics or monitor church growth. I am only a partner with the Chinese church, and like a child on Christmas Day, I am excited about unwrapping the gift that God is giving to Iran today through the Chinese underground house church.

The underground church in China has seen remarkable church growth for the last thirty years. Many sources estimate the conversion rate in China at several thousand every day. As the church continues to grow, the natural desire to send out evangelists and missionaries increases too.

Today, the Chinese church, which mainly consists of underground believers, has a vision to send out more than 100,000 missionaries into the region between China and Jerusalem. This area is often referred to as the 10/40 Window, a term that was used by Christian missionary strategist Luis Bush in 1990 in reference to countries located between 10 and 40 degrees north of the equator.

If you have not heard of the 10/40 Window, you should familiarize yourself with it immediately. This region contains the least evangelized people groups in the world and is notorious for extreme violence and persecution toward Christians. Two-thirds of the world's population and nine-tenths of the unreached people groups live in the 10/40 Window, but few mission organizations actually focus their efforts in this region.

According to the evangelical resource group the Traveling Team, on average, only 0.1 percent of Christian income in America is given to missions, and of that 0.1 percent, 87 percent goes toward mission work in areas that already have access to the Gospel. Only 1 percent of what is given to missions is channeled to the work with unreached peoples in the 10/40 Window.

To further emphasize the current status of outreach today, the Traveling Team points out that Christians are capable of providing all the funds needed to plant a church in each of the 6,900 unreached people groups with only 0.03 percent of their income.[1]

Christians are constantly praying for the fulfillment of the Great Commission, that God's Word would go forth to all the nations. But many in the Western church are not actively living out their faith. The Western church today has roughly three thousand times the financial resources and nine thousand times the manpower needed to fulfill the Great Commission.

The Chinese church, however, is starting to take the calling of Acts 1:8 and the command of Jesus in Matthew 28:18–20 very seriously.

Brother Joshua is a pastor in China in a network of about 5 million believers. He is leading the charge of sending missionaries into the 10/40 Window. "In China," he said, "we have been taken out of the frying pan of persecution and into the battlefields of Muhammad and Buddha. We have been led out of the slavery of Communism and into the battles with animism and Hinduism, and God is calling the leadership of China to go. It is not enough to have the vision of Back to Jerusalem. The vision alone is not a guarantee of victory."

Iran is right in the middle of the 10/40 Window and is the epitome of the unreached people groups in the region. Iran is considered a closed country and does not allow any open sharing of the Gospel message. The open distribution of Bibles or Christian materials is banned. Christian missionaries or mission organizations are not allowed to operate openly. Muslims are not allowed to convert. Iranian children cannot be proselytized. At the writing of this book, there is no legal church to serve the needs of the Iranian people.

The price for conversion is high, sometimes resulting in death.

If you want to share the Good News of Jesus in Iran, you will have no choice but to do so illegally. Some Christian organizations are not comfortable with illegal Christian activities. They feel that the ends do not justify the means.

Others are not comfortable with the idea of risking the lives of other people in order to preach about Jesus. Iran is full of hard choices when it comes to preaching the Gospel. It is a country that has kept missionaries at bay for generations. It is why Brother Joshua is focusing his efforts there. He knows that it will not be easy. "The best part about the people in Iran is that they know that Islam is their enemy," Joshua said while walking the streets of an Iranian city in 2013.

As I stood on the side of the road in Tehran and waited for the phone call from the Iranian underground house church leader, I couldn't help but notice the sheer number of young people rushing to and fro. Iran's population is relatively young. It is estimated that 70 percent or almost three-fourths of the population is under the age of thirty, and the majority of them lives in the cities.

Seventy percent of the population of Iran also live in urban areas, making cities like Tehran congested and polluted. Tehran is considered to be one of the most polluted cities in the world, but it is not the pollution that is stifling the development of the people—it's the government.

Prior to leaving my hotel, I had requested for the receptionist to arrange for a car to take me to Revolution Square. As I waited for the driver, the receptionist and I began to talk.

"I see from your passport that you travel a lot," she said. Upon checking into a hotel in Iran, the hotel staff will keep the passport of foreigners at the reception desk as a matter of policy, and you can only get it back when you check out. I could tell that my passport had been passed around to a very curious staff, who had more interest than merely keeping my passport secure.

"Yes," I replied. "I travel a lot for work and vacation with my family."

"I would love to travel, but it is not easy for an Iranian. Our government gives us many problems with countries around the world."

I smiled in acknowledgement of her words but did not give any indication of agreeing or disagreeing with her. As a policy, I never talk about the political matters of Iran while in Iran.

"I hate our government," she said abruptly. Her tone caught me off guard, but her words did not.

The underground house church worker who came to pick me up was also very vocal about his displeasure with the government, even though he used to be a member of the Iranian military, and he was barely able to hide his continual disgust at the way fellow Christians were treated in Iran.

While traveling and working in Iran, I have found that most young people are not only unhappy with their government, but they are also becoming increasingly vocal about it. A change is sweeping through Iran today, and it is one that is not being reported in international news. The country is facing a huge generational shift that is creating political instability for the current Islamic leadership. A battle is raging between the young Iranians and the Islamic leaders. Most of the young people in Iran, 70 percent of the population, are looking for answers they are not finding in Islam.

These young people between the ages of fourteen and twenty-eight have been living at home and listening to their parents; however, many of them are growing more independent in their thoughts. They have been born into and lived in a country that has been indoctrinated with Sharia Law. Many have seen their family and friends suffer for things they cannot even understand because of Islam, and they are fed up with the current situation.

There is a momentum today in Iran that we at Back to Jerusalem like to call ABI—Anything but Islam. The young people are hungry for truth and justice, and they are not finding either in Islam. The injustice that has been imposed on women in Iran is not sitting well with many of the younger people. The laws governing the use of the Internet are becoming less acceptable by the day. The constant and systematic monitoring and enforcement of the Islamic dress code at social entertainment venues is pushing people further away and isolating the young people. And draconian Islamic laws regulating basic travel, everyday commerce, and personal banking are choking the life out of the common citizen.

Iran has the potential for the largest Christian revival of any Muslim nation on earth, and some would say they are already experiencing the beginnings of it. Although currently there is a great lack of Christian leadership, workers, and materials, many Iranians are coming to Christ.

In the following chapters, we will explore the past and present church of Iran, how the Chinese are serving there, and how you can be a part of this vision and mission. This will be Iran as you have never seen it before, and you may never look at it the same way again.

1

A STRATEGY FOR IRAN

How many Christians would you say there are in Tehran?" I asked my friend from the underground house church in Iran.

"I don't know," he replied in his broken English.

"Well, how many fellowships would you say exist here in Tehran?" I tried again.

"I am not really sure."

"Okay, how do we know if there are Bibles needed here?"

"The Bibles are needed. So many believers need Bibles here," was the response.

"Great. So how many Bibles should we get?"

"A lot."

His response was one of the most honest I had come across. At least he admitted he did not know. Many Iranian "experts" who are not living in Iran speculate about conditions and needs, but there's really no way to confirm them.

The more I work with the church in Iran, the more complicated things seem to get. So the question is, how can we help? How do we pray? What can we do?

How do we deal with Iran?

This is not a unique problem for Back to Jerusalem missionaries from China. Iran presents problems that some of the most highly paid experts around the world don't know how to address. Governments, diplomats, mega-companies, and militaries have spent billions of dollars paying for advice and employing strategies. But no amount of money, expertise, or diplomacy seems to work. Many have tried and failed and wanted to wash their hands of the country, but Iran is not a place that should be forgotten or ignored. It is one of the oldest civilizations in the world, has the second most powerful military in the Middle East, and is the proud owner of a lot of underground desert black gold, also known as oil. Iran has the second largest oil reserves in the world and is able to pump more than four million barrels per day.

No one should presume they understand Iran based on their limited knowledge through the media. Not only are most of our preconceptions about Iran wrong, but even our analysis after study and exposure is most likely skewed as well.

The situation in Iran for Iranian Christians and Jews is deteriorating. Iranian Christians are imprisoned, beaten, and killed for their faith in Jesus Christ. Often they are whisked away in the middle of the night and subjected to torture before they are even given a trial.

Christians have not been the only ones threatened by the Islamic government of Iran. Iran's neighbors have been held hostage to its nuclear development. Israel has taken every diplomatic and economic route in its power to neutralize the threat, but nothing has seemed to work.

Iran has one of the largest numbers of executions in the world, carried out according to Islamic law. If the Iranian government has so little respect for Iranian lives, why would the lives of others matter to them? With a military supported by a wealth of natural resources and carrying out the commands of an Islamic cleric that believes in the absolute authority of the Koran, no one is safe. The leaders are obsessed with the complete and absolute annihilation of Israel and anyone else who gets in their way.

Iran's nuclear program has the world grasping for ideas to ensure security because no one believes that Iran is developing a nuclear program for energy needs alone, especially because Iran is sitting on one of the world's largest oil reserves.

The world community has spent billions of dollars on programs and sanctions to deal with Iran. They have summoned their best experts and pooled together more resources than there have been available at any given time in history, but all to no avail.

Iran is threatening the future of the world, especially the future of the next generation. The threat from Iran is getting worse, and the most powerful and wealthiest countries in the world do not know how to stop it.

The United Nations is helpless. Their policies of diplomacy and empty threats do not work. They have been a paper tiger in their dealings with Iran.

There is a joke about the United Nations (UN). Once, the UN saw a meteorite coming toward the earth, so the Secretary of the UN sent a message warning the meteorite to change course. The meteorite continued on its trajectory toward earth.

The UN then sent a "strongly worded" letter from the world community warning the meteorite that a failure to change course might result in a more strongly worded letter in the future.

When the meteorite continued on its trajectory, the UN issued a series of economic sanctions against the meteorite. When the meteorite finally crashed into the earth, the UN issued a statement of tolerance and understanding from all nations and made the meteorite a member of the UN Security Council. This joke is reflective of the ineffectiveness of the United Nations in its dealings with Iran.

The world has tried many different methods, but there is still one method that has not been employed yet.

Jesus told us in Matthew 5:43–45, "You have heard that it was said, 'You shall love your neighbor and hate your enemy.' But I say to you, Love your enemies and pray for those who persecute you, so that you may be sons of your Father who is in heaven."

Maybe the world governments are fighting the wrong fight. "For we do not wrestle against flesh and blood, but against the authorities, against the cosmic powers over the present darkness, against the spiritual forces of evil in the heavenly places," warned the apostle Paul in Ephesians 6:12.

For generations, governments have been fighting the battle in their own strength, and what good has it done?

Since 1979, sanction after sanction has been imposed on Iran, and military option after military option has been employed, but the situation has not improved.

US military operations take place on a regular basis on the Iraqi and Afghan borders of Iran to keep its military in check.

Has Iran been intimidated? Has its nuclear ambitions been abandoned or delayed?

What if, instead of bombs, we send Bibles?

What if, instead of soldiers, we send missionaries?

What if, instead of making war with Iran, we send the best gift of Love that has ever been given to mankind?

Back to Jerusalem missionaries are being sent from the most rural areas of China to Iran. The goal of the Back to Jerusalem vision of the Chinese underground house church is to launch a different type of offensive.

The Chinese underground house church is not fighting the Iranians. They are joining their brothers and sisters on the other side of enemy lines. Iran is not enemy territory; it is territory that has been occupied by the enemy. There is a difference. The Iranians are friends who are living in occupied territory.

Blessing your enemy is not to be confused with passive ministry. This does not mean there will not be confrontations, and it does not mean that there will not be fierce opposition. Blessing and loving are not the same as appeasement. Appeasement is the opposite of love. Appeasement is essentially about self-preservation. Love, true love, is willing to be sacrificial.

But let us step back and evaluate the idea of sending missionaries into Iran. Is it just naïve to believe that a Bible and well-meaning intentions can make a real difference in Iran?

Is it nothing more than senseless suicide to embark on such a seemingly futile mission?

According to Robert Woodberry, a sociologist currently doing research at the political science department of the National University of Singapore, missionaries have been pivotal change agents in transforming societies for the better throughout history. Woodberry's research gives conclusive evidence that missionaries in the last three hundred years have been the most significant factors in creating healthy societies. According to an article in *Christianity Today*, "Areas where Protestant missionaries had a significant presence in the past are on average more economically developed today, with comparatively better health, lower infant mortality, lower corruption, greater literacy, higher educational attainment (especially for women), and more robust membership in nongovernmental associations."

Why would Iran be any different? What makes Christians think they must wait for diplomatic channels to make life better before they can truly start to work? What if the answer is the other way around?

Woodberry's ground-breaking research is already sending shockwaves throughout academia. If his conclusions are true, then the work of missionaries is not for the salvation of lost souls alone. It will be the single most important factor in ensuring the health of nations, which will in turn benefit future generations.

One morning, in a windowless, dusty computer lab lit by florescent bulbs, Woodberry ran the first big test. After he finished prepping the statistical program on his computer, he clicked "Enter" and then leaned forward to read the results.

"I was shocked," says Woodberry. "It was like an atomic bomb. The impact of missions on global democracy was huge. I kept adding variables to the model—factors that people had been studying and writing about for the past 40 years—and they all got wiped out. It was amazing.

I knew, then, I was on to something really important."
Woodberry already had historical proof that mission-
aries had educated women and the poor, promoted wide-
spread printing, led nationalist movements that empowered
ordinary citizens, and fueled other key elements of democ-
racy. Now the statistics were backing it up: Missionaries
weren't just part of the picture. They were central to it.[1]

Iran is overflowing in resources, but their people are dying from poverty. Iran has a long, rich history of culture and freedom, but their people are suffering at the hands of dictators. The Iranians did not choose to be born in Iran. The Iranians did not choose to be born into Islam. They are living in a nightmare, and only the name of the Lord can save them, for "whosoever shall call upon the name of the Lord shall be saved. How then shall they call on him in whom they have not believed? and how shall they believe in him of whom they have not heard? and how shall they hear without a preacher? And how shall they preach, except they be sent?" (Romans 10:13–15 KJV).

According to Woodberry's research, America is not freer than Iran because Americans merely have a better system of government or more efficient economic engine. And Americans are not any smarter or more hardworking than the Iranians.

Laws do not create freedom. Free countries are not *just* the result of legislative efforts. China has laws guaranteeing freedom of press. North Korea has freedom of religion. Cuba has freedom of speech. But obviously there is something missing that does not translate those laws into actual freedom for the citizens of those countries.

If laws, systems, or the hard work and effort of the citizenry alone do not create free countries, then what does? Woodberry's research points to the work of Christian missionaries as the primary factor in determining the level of freedom experienced in any given country. Missionaries brought with them a set of moral values and ethical practices that helped create an environment conducive to freedom. Their beliefs led them to spread infectious and radical ideas of equality regardless of sex, race, religion, or economic standing.

Christian missionaries acted on their beliefs and ideals in tangible ways by helping the poor, protecting the weak, and reaching the lost. They build hospitals, schools, and printing presses. As people received and accepted the message of the missionary, those new Christian ideas directly contributed to justice and impacted the interpretation of laws and the enforcement of them.

Missionaries have been preaching this for years, but Woodberry's research has now produced statistical date to back up their claims. However, the missionary's message has only this much power when it is received by the receiver. Nothing can be forced upon the hearers of the message.

Just as God sent Jonah to Nineveh to call the people to repent and follow Him, the message only had power equal to (and not greater than) the willingness of the people to receive it.

North Korea and South Korea are populated by people with the same history, culture, language, and physical features. They live on the very same isolated peninsula, but the two countries could not be more different.

North Korea persecutes and kills their Christians. They have destroyed churches and Christian literature. In South Korea, Christians have freedom and protection. Envoys from South Korea are sent on a regular basis to Israel in a show of support and solidarity with the Jewish people.

As a result, science, academia, medicine, business, and even leisure activities have flourished in South Korea. In North Korea, these things have withered and are on life support.

Back to Jerusalem missionaries from China have seen firsthand the difference God's truth can make in their nation. I believe the unprecedented rate of conversion in China has resulted in the economic, political, and social freedoms they currently enjoy.

There is a strong belief that the way to heal Iran is no different. Author Reza Safa of *The Coming Fall of Islam in Iran: Thousands of Muslims Find Christ in the Midst of Persecution*, wisely said, "Do not slap a man who has more than four brothers! If you slap one, you must be ready to slap them all. Are we ready to wage a war against all 1.3 billion Muslims?"[2]

Iran can't be saved by bombs and bullets. There are not enough soldiers in the world to correct the problem in Iran or to protect the world from the growing threat. Fighting the Iranian threat with military supremacy only exacerbates the problem.

The only feasible and rational option is to follow the words of Christ, to show love and bless the Iranians.

2

IRAN IN THE BIBLE

The God of Abraham, Isaac, and Jacob is not new to Iran, and neither is Christianity. Those opposing the work of the Back to Jerusalem missionaries might argue that Christianity is a foreign religion to Iran, but it is in fact Islam that is a foreign religion.

While reading this, it is important to keep in mind that the Bible is not a Western book. It was written in the Middle East. In fact, the book of Esther takes place entirely in Iran.

Iran, or the Persian Empire, is mentioned repeatedly in the Old Testament because the Middle East was ruled by Persia during much of that time.

One can better understand Iranian history by reading the Bible, and one can better understand the Bible by studying Iranian history.

Christianity is not new to Iran, and neither are the concepts. Christian influence has been in Iran since the beginning of the church. Elamites (Persians), Medes, and Parthians were present on the day of Pentecost in the book of Acts (2:9). Christianity was introduced to Iran long before Islam reached Persian soil.

Famous biblical figures believed to be buried in Iran include Esther, Daniel, Cyrus the Great, Darius the Great, and the disciple Thaddeus.

The bones of the prophet Daniel are believed to be buried in Iran not far from the old capital city of Susa. According to records preserved by both the Jews and the Muslims, the grand tomb of the prophet Daniel still stands—it has outlasted the fortress and the ancient capital of Susa. Records also reveal that invading Muslim forces found a mummy with the symbol of a man between two lions at the tomb and that it was preserved against the wishes of the commanding officers.

Many people believe that the magi of the nativity came from Iran and took the message of the birth of Christ back to Iran. That would mean that the magi would have been the first Christian missionaries to Iran. This also means that the Iranians would have been among the first to worship Jesus the Christ!

For historians, the Bible is actually one of the most accurate recordings of some of the most influential nations of the ancient world, including Iran. The Bible is a treasure chest of information overflowing with nuggets and gems of names, places, practices, and cultural references. Some academics loathe the fact that the Bible is so incredibly accurate and reliable because of the secular desire to cast doubts on the authenticity of the Bible. However, when talking about Iran, there are few resources that are as well kept as the biblical records. Whenever new findings contradict biblical records, a new finding eventually surfaces to correspond with the Bible account.

Genealogies and references to time periods in the Bible are unique in all of the religious writings of the world. For many who are reading the Bible for the first time, it might seem like a bore and completely unnecessary to list who was whose father and what land was conquered by whom and what day of the month of the year and what happened during whose reign. However, biblical authors took painstaking efforts to research, document, and share the story of God's redemptive plan throughout history so the people could look back and have the evidence to show actual events had occurred.

I remember taking a world religions course at Palomar College in San Marcos, California. The professor was a long-haired Buddhist, a white guy who wore cowboy boots and sat cross-legged on his desk while he taught.

As he recounted the story of the Jews leaving Egypt, he told it as a comical story that was as unbelievable as a cartoon (which struck me as odd because he shared the stories of the Hindu gods as if they were real events that could be traced in history). The class of about thirty students laughed along with him at the impossibility of the event as recorded in the book of Exodus.

I raised my hand and asked, "Well, weren't the Jews slaves in Egypt?" Not waiting for an answer, I continued on. "Are they still slaves in Egypt? If not, then how did they break free? A war is not recorded in the Egyptian records, or is it?"

No answer.

It would be difficult to believe that one day the Egyptians felt compassionate and allowed all the slaves to leave. "Did the Egyptians record how the Jews left Egypt and broke away from slavery? That was a migration of several million slaves."

"No, we have no records from the Egyptians."

"Well then, it is a fact that the Jews were slaves in Egypt. It is also a fact that they are no longer slaves in Egypt. And as far as we know, the Jews were the only ones to record how this factual event took place."

Even if one does not believe in the biblical record of how the uneducated and unorganized Jews left Egypt, the fact that they did was miraculous. Then there's the crossing of the Red Sea, the pillar of fire illuminations, and the water and manna that sustained the Jews in the most difficult and harsh environment known to mankind. If the Bible is not true, then we must find another explanation, but another explanation would need to be as equally miraculous for the Jews to have survived!

The records of biblical history and its validity matter when we look at the history of Iran.

Modern-day Iran is first mentioned in the Bible as Elam, named after one of the sons of Shem, the son of Noah. Later, Iran is referred to as Persia. For the purpose of discussion, when discussing biblical Persia, we will refer to it as Iran. It might help to clarify the difference by viewing Iran as anti-Semitic and distinct from Persia.

Of all of the empires that have ever ruled over the earth, few did more for the Jews than the Iranians. The Iranians rescued the Jews from slavery in Babylon and allowed them to return to their homeland and even contributed to the rebuilding of the Holy Temple of Jehovah.

The Jewish people had forgotten their Lord God and had abandoned His teachings. God's protection was no longer upon them, and as a consequence, the northern tribes of Israel were conquered and taken into slavery by the Assyrians. Eventually the southern tribes of Judah were defeated by Babylon and captured as slaves.

The temple was destroyed, and the Jewish people were forced to walk more than four hundred miles from Judah to modern-day Iraq, where they were beaten, raped, killed, and sold as slaves. Seventy years later, God moved the king of Iran, and with His blessing, the king conquered Babylon.

On October 29, 540 BC, crowds filled the ancient city of Babylon waiting to see the man who had just overthrown their king and conquered their land. The famous city of Babylon, which was one of the most powerful city centers in the known world, fell into the hands of King Cyrus with very little resistance.

Those who lined the streets that day waited to hear from their new master to see what their fate would be. Every battle that had ever been fought in the known world at that time naturally resulted in the enslavement of women and children, execution of men, and untamed looting and destruction.

Instead, the Iranian king Cyrus did something that had never been done before by a conquering king. He showed mercy and justice. He abolished slavery and liberated the captives of those he conquered.

Not only did the Iranian king set the Jews free, but he supported the return of an estimated forty-two thousand Jews to their homeland in Jerusalem. He restored to the Jews all that the Babylonians had taken from them. They traveled back to their homeland carrying silver and gold. The Iranian king himself gave gold and silver to the Jews to take back with them on their journey (Ezra 1:7–11). This sparked the rebuilding of the temple that had been destroyed and desecrated by the Babylonians.

God gave the founder and king of Iran, King Cyrus, a huge task that was unparalleled by any other in Gentile history. King Cyrus was anointed (Isaiah 45:1) to deliver the Jews and rebuild the city of Jerusalem. More promises were recorded regarding the Gentile king Cyrus of Iran than most of the other kings who served Israel.

In 1879, an Assyro-British archaeologist Hormuzd Rassam discovered a baked-clay cylinder in Akkadian language with cuneiform script in the foundation of the Marduk temple of Babylon. Today it's in the British Museum of London.

This cylinder describes how King Cyrus conquered the powerful city of Babylon and how his army marched into the city to claim his place as king. Cyrus considered himself to be chosen by a supreme God as recorded in the book of Isaiah in the Bible.

The cylinder also proclaimed racial, linguistic, and religious equality for all. Slaves were set free, and laborers were paid wages. Like the justice of Yahweh as recorded in the Old Testament, Cyrus promoted respect for humanity and justice for the oppressed. This earned him the overwhelming support of his subjects.

The writings found on the cylinder have been translated into all six official UN languages, and a replica is kept at the United Nations headquarters in New York City.

Daniel 6:25–28 records how Cyrus's son, King Darius, followed in the footsteps of his father:

> *Then king Darius wrote to all the peoples, nations, and languages that dwell in all the earth: "Peace be multiplied to you. I make a decree, that in all my royal domin-*

ion people are to tremble and fear before the God of Daniel, for he is the living God, enduring forever; his kingdom shall never be destroyed, and his dominion shall be to the end. He delivers and rescues; he works signs and wonders in heaven and on earth, he who has saved Daniel from the power of the lions." So this Daniel prospered in the reign of Darius and the reign of Cyrus the Persian.

The Persian Empire stretched from Egypt and the borders of Greece, through the Middle East, to Pakistan, India, and Central Asia, and to the borders of China. This territory includes modern-day Egypt, Jordan, Iraq, Kuwait, Oman, UAE, Iran, Lebanon, Turkey, Armenia, Azerbaijan, Turkmenistan, Uzbekistan, Tajikistan, Afghanistan, Kazakhstan, India, and even the birth place of Islam, Saudi Arabia. This is the 10/40 Window of today! These are the hardest to reach areas of the world that severely restrict and prohibit the spread of the Word of God. However, during the days of Daniel, every tribe, nation, and tongue in the 10/40 Window was able to hear that the God of Daniel was the one true God!

After King Cyrus died, conflict occurred when the people who did not follow the one true God were not allowed to participate in the rebuilding of the Jewish temple out of concern that they would lay the foundations for false ideology and teachings as they laid the foundation with brick and mortar.

They complained to the new king of Iran, and an order was issued to stop all construction on the temple. This order remained in effect until King Darius rose to power.

During the reign of King Darius, construction resumed again on the temple. After the reign of King Darius came that of Xerxes.

Artaxerxes, king of kings, to Ezra the priest, the scribe of the Law of the God of heaven peace. And now I make a decree that anyone of the people of Israel, or their priests or Levites in my kingdom, who freely offers to go

*to Jerusalem, may go with you. For you are sent by the
king and his seven counselors to make inquiries about Judah and Jerusalem according to the Law of your God,
which is in your hand, and also to carry the silver and
gold that the king and his counsellors have freely offered
to the God of Israel, whose dwelling is in Jerusalem, with
all the silver and gold that you shall find in the whole
province of Babylonia, and with the freewill offerings of
the people and the priests, vowed willingly for the house
of their God that is in Jerusalem. (Ezra 7:12–17)*

The king of Iran sent the Jews out with a promise of all the
gold and silver they could find so that they could use it for the
temple, and if it was more than enough, they could use the rest
according to the will of Jehovah (Ezra 7:18). The king opened up
his own treasure house and told the Jews to take what they needed.

Verse 23 reads, "Whatever is decreed by the God of heaven,
let it be done in full for the house of the God of heaven, for lest his
wrath be against the realm of the king and his sons."

Here, in his decree, the most powerful king of the known
world was making it clear that he fully acknowledged the powerful God of the Jews and did not want to oppose anything that He
commanded. This is a remarkable and rare story where the king's
treasury was opened up, not for the people of Iran, but for the Jewish people.

Furthermore, the Iranian king made it against the law for any
clergy members or temple workers to be taxed or charged any toll.

This was an extraordinary measure, and it was the law throughout the entire kingdom.

On top of that, the king ordered all judges and court workers to be trained in the Law of God so that justice could be defined accordingly. Anyone who did not obey the Law of God
and the law of Iran was ordered to be punished and, in some
cases executed!

For all of hardships the Iranians had endured, it had been promised in Jeremiah 49:39, "But in the latter days I will restore the fortunes of Elam, declares the LORD."

This short glimpse of the biblical history of Iran provides a completely different view of Iran from the most recent news broadcasts of BBC or CNN. There is a strong history connecting the Iranian people to the will of God. God used the Iranian people in a very mighty way in the past, and He can do so again.

3

ESTHER, THE IRANIAN BOOK OF THE BIBLE

Esther is one of the strangest books in the Bible, but it is pivotal to the story of survival of God's people, and Iran plays a central role. To fully understand the book of Esther, one must first understand the Iranian context in which it occurred.

Many scholars have argued that the book of Esther should have never been canonized or added to the Bible at all.

This book of the Bible does not even carry a Jewish name. The name *Esther* is Iranian. It is thought to mean "star."

Take note of the uniqueness of this book. It is not referenced anywhere else in the Bible. Jesus never quoted from it. None of the main characters pray in the book of Esther, and there are no supernatural miracles performed. Nowhere in the entire book of Esther is God mentioned. God doesn't lead anyone, speak to anyone, or give signs to anyone. We do not see Esther keeping any of the kosher laws of the Jewish people or openly celebrating any of the Jewish festivities. And the heroin of the story, Esther, is a woman who is selected for her beauty, not her piety.

The book of Esther is not religious in the traditional sense, and many Christian readers might actually feel uncomfortable with its lack of overt connection to God. The Qumran Community did not include the book of Esther in their library, and the Jews who wrote the Septuagint inserted prayers from Mordecai because the lack of prayer was difficult for them to accept. The Greek Septuagint retained these prayers, although they were not included in the Jewish canon.

But it was not by chance that all these events took place in the book of Esther. Again God used an Iranian king to stop the destruction of the Jewish people. Prior to this event, the Jews had turned their backs on God and as a result were taken as slaves to Babylon—modern-day Iraq.

There they were set free by King Cyrus, but during the time of Esther, they were still foreigners. The king who now ruled was named Xerxes, and his trusted advisor, Haman, is one of the key players in the story of Esther and how God used her to save the Jewish people. It is important to know who Haman is in the book of Esther because it is not a coincidence that he is the one who tried to destroy the Jews.

Haman was an Agagite (Esther 3:1), and the explanation for his hatred for Esther's cousin, Mordecai, who was Jewish, actually goes back much further than the book of Esther. Haman would not have existed to threaten the Jews if King Saul had carried out the will of God.

Amalekites were known as a nomadic people who regularly attacked the Jewish people. They are thought to be descendents of Esau, the brother of Jacob. In 1 Samuel 15, God clearly appointed Saul as the king of Israel and commanded him to lead the people against the Amalekites and destroy every living thing. Saul was ordered to kill every man, woman, child, livestock, and house pet: "Now go and smite Amalek devote to destruction all that they have. Do not spare them, but kill both man and woman, child and infant, ox and sheep, camel and donkey" (15:3).

But King Saul did not do what the Lord had commanded. Instead, he spared the king, Agag. Haman was an Agagite from the lineage of King Agag. As an Agagite, Haman was naturally disposed to hate the Jews because of the murder of his tribe. In King Xerxes's court, Haman was the equivalent of what we might call a prime minister or chief of staff. Everyone bowed down before him. Everyone except Mordecai.

When Mordecai didn't bow down to Haman, Haman took it

personally. Mordecai was a Jew, and in Haman's eyes, Mordecai was the worst kind of Jew. He was a Benjamite from the tribe of Kish, which meant he was from the line of King Saul, whose father was Kish. So here were the descendents of Saul facing the evil tribe of the Amalekite king—again. This conflict would not be happening a second time if King Saul had been obedient to God's commands.

Even though Mordecai was the one who reported a plot to assassinate the king in Esther 2, Haman was given the highest seat of honor and rose to become one of the most powerful people in the most powerful empire of the world. There is no record of Mordecai openly defying Haman. He was not actively leading a revolt. But when he refused to bow to Haman, Haman was offended. His anger got the better of him, and he devised a plan to kill not just Mordecai but every single Jew in the known world.

Mordecai represented the misery of Haman's ancestors, so Haman went to the Iranian king and asked him to permit the genocide of the Jewish people. The Iranian king agreed and signed Haman's decree. Thus a decree was sent from Iran throughout the known world to eliminate the Jewish race from the face of the earth. Because of the efficiency of the communication system that was invented by the Iranians, it would only be a matter of time before every kingdom knew about and planned to enforce Haman's scheme.

Esther had been chosen to be the queen of Iran without the court knowing she was a Jew. She was living as an Iranian, and she spoke like, acted like, and obviously looked like an Iranian, but she was not. Beneath her royalty and beauty, she was a Jew. When Esther's cousin heard about the order approved by the king to exterminate the Jewish people, he was grieved and sent a message to Esther through a servant:

> *Mordecai also gave him a copy of the written the decree issued in Susa for their destruction, that he might*

show it to Esther and explain it to her and command her
to go to the king to beg for his favor and plead with him
her people. . . .

Then Esther spoke to Hathach and commanded him to
go to Mordecai and say, "All the king's servants and the
people of the king's provinces know that if any man or
woman goes to the king inside the inner court without being
called, there is but one law to be put to death, except the
one to whom the king holds out the golden scepter, so that
he may live. But as for me; I I have not been called to come
in to the king these thirty days. (Esther 4:8, 10–11)

Esther, the one whom most people believed to be Iranian, was
now asked to go in front of the king unannounced and plead for
the lives of her people, the Jews. This was no small matter. The
Iranian king was known to have a harsh temper.

King Xerxes led the Iranians to fight the Greeks. In order to
cross from Asia to Europe, the troops had to cross the sea. The
area was only about a mile wide, and King Xerxes decided that the
Iranian army engineers would build a bridge one mile long so that
the troops could cross over to Greece.

After the bridge was built, the troops attempted to cross, but the
water rose up and destroyed the bridge. Xerxes was so angry that he
ordered all of the engineers to be beheaded and then commanded
troops to walk out into the water and use their whips an lash the
water three hundred times to punish the water for its disobedience.

Esther's fear of approaching King Xerxes without proper pro-
tocol was completely justified, but Mordecai sent a stern message
to Esther:

"Do not think to yourself that in the king's palace you
will escape any more than all the other Jews. For if you
keep silent at this time, relief and deliverance will rise for
the Jews from another place, but you and your father's

house will perish. And who knows whether you have not come to the kingdom for such a time as this?" (Esther 4:13–14).

Upon seeing the desperation of the situation and the urgency of her cousin's words, Esther decided to act, even if it meant losing her life. She acknowledged the possibility when she said, "If I perish, I perish" (Esther 4:16).

There was very little time to spare. The size of the Iranian empire was immense, as it controlled present-day Egypt, Saudi Arabia, Israel, Jordan, Iraq, Turkey, Armenia, Azerbaijan, Turkmenistan, Uzbekistan, Tajikistan, Afghanistan, Pakistan, Kazakhstan, and India. But nothing traveled faster than the Iranian postal system. Messages would be sent out by riders who would ride to predesignated posts where fresh horses were waiting for them.

A system of visual signals was also developed so Iranians could communicate, one post with another, using light signals.

Esther and the Jewish people were at a serious disadvantage. She could not wait for the king to call her into his presence. She would have to figure a way to have an audience with the king.

Even if Esther lived to speak before the king, there would be another problem. No command given by an Iranian king and signed with his ring could ever be revoked (Esther 8:8). Not even the king could reverse a decision he had made. This is in line with the infallible nature that the people attributed to the king.

However, Esther was able to convince the king that an injustice had been done, and although he could not revoke his decision to have the Jews destroyed, he did give them the possibility of survival:

. . . Saying that the king allowed the Jews who were in every city to gather and defend their lives, to destroy, to kill, and to anninilate any armed forces of any people or province that might attack them, children and women included, and to plunder their goods, on one day through-

> *out all the provinces of King Ahasuerus, on the thirteenth day of the twelfth month, which is the month of Adar. A copy of what was written was to be issued as a decree in every province, being pubicly displayed to all peoples, and the Jews were to be ready on that day to take vengence on their enemies. (Esther 8:11–13)*

Basically, the Iranian king issued a decree similar to the Second Amendment found in the Constitution of the United States—the right to bear arms. The king was saying, "I can't stop people from trying to kill you, but I give you the right to fight back." The king allowed the Jews to stand up and fight anyone who would try to assault them, their families, or their property.

So the Jews gathered together and fought against those who attacked them.

Then the Iranian king had Haman and his ten sons hanged in the gallows. A decree was sent all over the Iranian kingdom that called the Jews to always remember this event with grand feasts and gifts to the poor. This event was called Purim, which is derived from the Iranian word *Pur* or "to cast lots" (Esther 9:24), indicating that the people who had cast lots or gambled against the Jews had lost.

This is an important part of Iranian and Jewish history and is still celebrated among the Jewish people today.

4
IRAN'S FIRST CHRISTIANS

Iran is a Muslim country, and as such, some interesting laws currently exist. For instance, it is illegal for a man to have a mullet. A mullet is a Western-style haircut that was made infamous by American country singer Billy Ray Cyrus. If you have ever seen a mullet haircut, this might not seem like such a bad idea.

Ponytails are also an illegal hairstyle for men. If the police see someone with a ponytail, they are authorized to give a trim on the spot. If someone is a repeat offender, they can be arrested and fined. It's also illegal for a man to wear too much gel, have hair that is excessively long, or have spiked hair.

Most would actually agree that the mullet is not attractive, but imagine a country where it's illegal for men to have a certain hairstyle. Any barber shop that is an accomplice to such hairstyles can lose their business license and have the doors to their business shut.

There is an official list of hairstyles that the Islamic government has approved. To rid the country of "decadent Western cuts," Iran's Ministry of Culture produced a catalogue of haircuts that meet government approval.

If this seems strange, think of the distrust for those who wear a neck tie with their suit, which is another offense that can be quickly translated as colluding with the enemy.

These silly laws are the result of an Islamic regime that is obsessed with controlling every aspect of every Iranian citizen's life. The majority of the people one finds on the street in any large metropolitan city in Iran would share their dissatisfaction with these laws if given the chance.

Many people around the world think Iran has always been Islamic and assume that it always will be because it is in their culture. There are some who feel that introducing Christ to Iranians is pushing Western religion on Persians and that they should be left alone. However, Islam is not the culture of the Iranians. Islam came from the Arabic culture. Iranians are not Arabic; they are Persian, and historically Persians were not Islamic.

Christianity has been a part of Iranian culture for far longer than Islam, and from a practical standpoint, Christianity is actually much more cohesive to the Iranian culture than Islam. I will explain more about that later, but for now, it is important to understand that Christianity was in Iran from the very beginning. Acts 2:4–9 says:

> *And they were all filled with the Holy Spirit and began to speak in other tongues as the Spirit gave them utterance.*
> *Now there were dwelling in Jerusalem Jews, devout men from every nation under heaven. And at this sound the multitude came together, and they were bewildered, because each one was hearing them speak in his own language. And they were amazed and astonished, saying, "Are not all these who are speaking Galileans? And how is it that we hear, each of us in his own native language? Parthians and Medes and Elamites and residents of Mesopotamia, Judea and Cappadocia, Pontus and Asia."*
> *(emphasis added)*

Parthians, Medes, and Elamites basically cover every major people group that make up the country of Iran.

Early Christian records show that Peter and Thomas actually preached the Gospel message to Iranians, as did Thaddeus and Bartholomew. Because of the Jewish population established in

Old Testament times, as was indicated in the previous chapters, there were still large Jewish centers in Iran when the first missionaries arrived.

When Jews who believed in Jesus arrived in new countries, the first place they would go to share the Good News was the synagogue. There were many Jewish centers in Iran for the Jews to congregate and hear the message of the preachers.

Even today, Iran still has the largest Jewish population in the Muslim world.

One of the reasons why many Iranians gravitated to the message of Jesus Christ might be because of their early belief in Zoroastrianism.

Zoroastrianism is one of the most notable religions in the history of Iran and is still deeply rooted in the Iranian culture. Interestingly enough, Islam has failed to snuff it out completely. Although it is known that Zoroastrianism was the main religion of Iran, it is debatable when the founding prophet of the religion, Zoroaster, actually lived. Many believe that it was between 1,000 and 600 BC.

According to tradition, followers of Zoroaster believed Zoroaster didn't come to start a new religion, but instead to bring people back to the faith of the ancient fathers. Cyrus the Great, the Iranian king, was the first ruler of Iran who ordained Zoroastrianism as the official religion. This is the same Cyrus who liberated the Jews and helped rebuild the temple of God.

It should be noted that Zoroastrianism shares much with Christianity:

1. The concepts of heaven and hell
2. A judgment day
3. Virgin birth
4. Resurrection
5. Eternal damnation in hell for the souls of the wicked

Followers of the Zoroastrian faith eventually persecuted Christians in Iran, but not before their beliefs opened up many doors.

Shortly after the Great Commission was commanded by Jesus, Rome went on a killing spree, making Christians the main target of their rampage. Christians around the known world traveled far and wide to seek refuge, safety, and protection in Iran. Thousands of Iranians embraced Christianity.

Iran benefited from the Christians. Many were professional tradesmen who were capable of large-scale construction projects. Many were trained in medicine, education, and economics and brought a wealth of knowledge to the Iranian people. Many were also involved in the lucrative silk production that brought much needed economic trade as well as financial stability.

Although most people acknowledge that Christianity spread throughout Iran in the early years, very few people actually know that Iran was once an official Christian country, though only for a brief time.

For more than four hundred years, between the ninth and fourteenth centuries, Nestorianism was the largest sector of Christianity in the world.

John Nestorius, who advanced the doctrine, was born in Germanicia, in modern-day Turkey (most of which was owned by Iran under the Sasanian Empire), not far from the border of modern-day Syria and about four hundred miles west of the border of present-day Iran.

The Nestorian doctrine has been debated because it was thought to have denied the divinity of Christ. This is rooted in the doctrine's emphasis of the term "Virgin Mary" over the use of "Mary Mother of God" (*Theotokos*) as Nestorians believed it was impossible for a woman to be the mother of God, who is eternal. However, these teachings were condemned by the first Council of Ephesus in 431, which maintained that Jesus is God, Mary was Jesus' mother, therefore Mary is the mother of God. The council's condemnation led to widespread rejection and persecution of anyone following the Christian doctrine of Nestorius. Today most scholars acknowledge that the classical view opposing Nestorius was the erroneous interpretation deliberately spread by the opponents within the Catholic Church at the Council of Ephesus.

The Christian believers in Iran welcomed these persecuted Christians from the Roman Catholic Church with wide-open arms. Many in the church in Iran did adopt the Nestorian doctrines, which became known as the Nestorian Church.

Iran was an empire that gave comfort and security to persecuted Christians.

Many Christians in the West saw Iran's acceptance of Nestorian teachings and the excommunicated followers as a challenge to them personally. Because of this, many use the terms the *Church of the East* and *Nestorians* interchangeably, although this is not entirely correct, as each group had different views that distinguished them from the Roman Church and Western Christianity.

The Church of the East was known as the largest in the world in terms of geography because it reached into so many areas. The church could not have come at a better time in Iran, because the Sasanian Empire, the ruling empire, ran most of the Eastern world. The Sasanian Empire of Iran encompassed modern-day Iran, Iraq, Bahrain, Kuwait, Oman, Qatar, UAE, Syria, Lebanon, Palestine, Jordan, Israel, Armenia, Georgia, Azerbaijan, Egypt, Turkey, Afghanistan, Uzbekistan, Tajikistan, Yemen, and Pakistan. In the areas that they did not control, their economic and military influence was certainly felt. With a church firmly established in Iran, with centers in every major financial city, the church began to boldly reach the farthest areas of the world.

The conquest of Islam put an end to the Christian advances Iran was making throughout the world. The impact of Islam was not immediate, but after the conquest of Iran was complete, the status of Christians among the ruling Muslims deteriorated.

No one could have predicted that the largest church in the world at that time and the primary balance to the Roman Church in the West would be snuffed out by the Muslims. The freedoms that extended to all the polytheistic religions, Far Eastern religions, and even to the indigenous Zoroastrians would be abolished. The Jewish people would again become second-class citizens, far removed from the days of Esther.

From just a brief look at Christianity in Iran's history, one can quickly understand a couple of things. First, the church in Iran was not an afterthought. It was the farthest-reaching church in the world at that time in terms of geography. The mission endeavors and theological contributions were absolutely astounding.

Second, the church of Jesus Christ was firmly established in Iran long before the arrival of Islam. This dispels the idea that Iranian culture is automatically Muslim, as most believe today. Iran is neither culturally nor historically Islamic. The imposition of a religion doesn't automatically assume the adoption of the culture. The notion that Iran is entirely a Muslim country and this has always been the case and always will be the case is clearly a false one that is not supported by history.

America and their allies were victorious in the war with Japan, but that did not make Japan a Christian nation. The people retained their religious and cultural identity. America and their allies were technically victorious in their war with Afghanistan and Iraq. No one debated whether the people of Afghanistan or Iraq should be forced to be Christians, which was the dominant religion of the coalition. In fact, the coalition military was not allowed to proselytize or hand out Christian literature.

In 2012, American military personnel threw away and ultimately burned Bibles that were printed in the two most common Afghan languages amid concern the Bibles would be used to try to convert Afghans, a Defense Department spokesman reported.

Lt. Col. Mark Wright, the commanding officer in Afghanistan, said, "The decision was made that it was a 'force protection' measure to throw them [the Bibles] away, because if they did get out, it could be perceived by Afghans that the US government or the US military was trying to convert Muslims to Christianity."

Unfortunately, the Iranian people did not get this privilege when the Arabs invaded their country. They were forced to accept Islam, and today they are *still* being forced to accept Islam. But being forced to adopt a religion does not mean that is where their hearts are.

Third, unlike Islam, the Gospel message that spread to Iran was widely accepted by the people but was not brought by the sword. The Zoroastrian and Jewish communities that accepted Jesus into their lives did so willingly. They were not forced to accept beliefs as they were with Islam.

In fact, writings have been found by Zoroastrian officials, prior to and during the persecutions, compelling followers of Zoroaster's teachings to mimic the Christian charity and mercy in all things to win the Christians over. Islam did not give the Iranians a choice.

Islam did not come to Iran to give the Iranian people freedom; it came to hold the people captive and has done so since the first day it arrived on Persian soil. Prior to Islam, some estimate that there were as many as 9 million Christian believers living in Iran who were either enslaved, taxed, forced to convert, or killed when Muslims entered the region. As we shall learn later in chapter 7, the march of Islam into Iran was not a pretty one.

5

IRAN SENDS CHRISTIANS TO CHINA

Where is the road?" I asked the camera guy as our taxi driver drove over a small ditch trying to go from one dirt path to another. We were not the first people to drive to the Da Qin Pagoda, but it was starting to feel like it. The driver was yelling in Chinese. We were in a Chinese taxi that was obviously designed for urban transport, not dirt tracks.

"Dude, where are we?"

"I don't know." The cameraman laughed as we desperately tried to find a sign of historical reference.

We were outside of Xi'an, the ancient capital of China. Xi'an is a city of about 8 to 10 million people today. It is not a small town and we were not that far from the city center, but it felt as if we had just entered one of the most remote areas of China. We were bumping along the road looking for one of the most significant sights in all of China for Christians: the oldest church. It's over a thousand years old and was built by Iranians.

You might want to read that last sentence again. The things that Iran has been responsible for regarding Christian missions are absolutely mind blowing. The Iranian role in the history of missions in China can teach today's Chinese Back to Jerusalem missionaries so much.

When I traveled to Tehran for the first time after having served in China for several years, I was amazed at the things that I saw that were so closely related to China.

Like China, Iran is one of the oldest civilizations in the world. In the early days of civilization, both China and Iran were dealing with large urban populations, food sourcing, waste disposal, water sanitation, housing, government procedures, infrastructure building codes, public transportation, information decimation, and municipal law enforcement long before the rest of the world. Today China and Iran are run by revolutionary regimes. One is Islamic and the other is Communist, but the main participants of the revolutions in both cases were idealistic young college students.

Anyone who has traveled to the Pearl Market in Beijing or the main bazaar in Tehran would appreciate the loud, bustling chaos that is somehow typical of the excitement and energy of bargaining for the lowest price. The bazaar, like the street markets in China, is a place where no price is final until either the haggler or the vendor gives in.

Many of the Iranian apartment buildings look very similar to Communist era structures. During meals, guests are put in a seat of honor, like in China, often farthest from the door. If one does not have enough food for the guest, then the hosts immediately go out and get more.

Arranged marriages in Iran are very much like the ones arranged by parents in China.

The most celebrated holiday of the year in Iran is the Iranian New Year, celebrated in spring, when the Chinese New Year is also celebrated. During the New Year, both Iranians and the Chinese prepare huge feasts for their families.

Both the Chinese and Iranian New Year are based on the time of the equinox, or the equal division of day and night.

Iranians are well known for their gardens. In fact, the English word *paradise* comes from the Iranian word meaning "enclosed garden." Chinese gardens are also enclosed and are a place of peace and tranquility.

Both Iranians and Chinese are known for their poetry. Chinese proverbs are known throughout the world, as are Iranian poems. China is known as a country that persecutes Christians, but today it is also a country that is very much focused on Christian missions. In fact, the Chinese Christians have a vision to carry out one of the most aggressive and large-scale Christian mission outreaches the world has ever seen. The sending out of at least 100,000 missionaries is what they call the Back to Jerusalem vision.

The most visible Iranian symbols today are those that celebrate Islam, but history shows that the believers in Iran were once just as zealous as the Christians in China are today. The Silk Road cuts straight through Iran from China. And although it was once used to send goods from the east to the west, it was also used by the Christians in Iran to send missionaries from the west to the east—all the way to China.

The Nestorian Church, which existed during the Persian Empire, sent out more missionaries than almost any other church. These ambitious missionaries were planting churches throughout Central Asia, Tibet, Korea, India, Vietnam, Japan, and China.

Marco Polo made mention of the Christian communities he came in contact with as he documented his travels into the most hostile, untamed regions of the known world. Although he is noted as being the famous explorer, he was several hundred years behind the trailblazing Christians from Iran.

Iran is oddly a common theme in the mission of the disciples of Jesus. Even though Paul went west and Luke shared Paul's mission westward in the book of Acts, one of the twelve disciples, Simon the Zealot, is said to have been sawed in half in Suanir, Iran.

Two monasteries in the northern part of Iran, Saint Thaddeus and Saint Stephanos Monasteries, are said to be related to the history of the apostles Jude and Bartholomew bringing the Gospel to Iran. Thomas, also known as doubting Thomas, is said to have made contact with the Iranian church and obtained the support he needed to continue all the way to India.

There is another aspect of their identity that the Chinese and Iranians share that few people have noticed. The oldest surviving Christian church in China is claimed to have been built by the Nestorians from Iran, and the oldest surviving church in Iran was rebuilt by the Chinese!

When I read this for the first time, I was speechless. How could the oldest church in China be built by the Iranians and the oldest church in Iran be rebuilt by funding from a Chinese empress?

The answer is a long one. The majority of the Silk Road was within Iranian-controlled territory and provided the backbone for Christian growth in China. The Syrian Christians, the majority of the Nestorian push for many of the missions, were from the Iranian-controlled empire. The city at the center of much trade was Antioch, which is where the term *Christian* is first thought to have originated from. It was along the Silk Road that this term was used to identify those that followed Jesus.

The Iranians controlled the coasts east of the Persian Gulf to the Indian Ocean, and Christians from Iran were able to use these ocean routes to take missionaries to and fro on the southern route of the Iran-China Silk road.

During the Dark Ages of Europe, when the Roman Church was engrossed in deep theological turmoil, the Christians based out of the Iranian territories were focusing more on making new disciples. Unlike the Catholic Church, the Iranian Christians did not have the backing of an empire.

Like the Chinese Christians today, the Iranian Christians did not have the financial or military support of their government. This is an amazing similarity that is only now coming to light.

The Sasanian Dynasty sent many representatives from the headquarters in Susa to build the new city of Djondishapur, where the soon-to-be east-bound missionaries would receive their theological, academic, and in some cases, medical training. The medical training was second to none and was even said to have played a part in an Iranian missionary named Rimitsu leading a Japanese empress to Christ, which also led to the founding of a hospital, care facility, and orphanage as far east as Japan.

The Church of the East were strong believers in education. They attempted to start an education center with every congregation. These education centers were important for the spread of Christianity. The Christians who were being sent out from Iran were used to living in culturally and politically diverse countries where believers did not control the political spectrum. They had to live side by side with people from other faiths and were not looking to take political control, but they were looking to convert the hearts of man to the true Savior of the world regardless of politics. They had an urgency about their work.

These missionaries from Iran traveled on foot with only sandals on their feet. Those who did not take to the seas navigated the streams and mountains by land with only wooden staffs in their hands. They carried wooden woven baskets on their back that contained scriptures. They carried a cross to remind them of their mission through the hardship and walked all the way to China!

The Church of the East and their sacrifice for the Chinese is a story that is being told to the Back to Jerusalem missionaries in China today. The missionaries from Iran traveled six thousand miles to China without airplanes, Internet, money transfers, exchange vendors, mobile phones, or electronic Bibles. They traversed the highest mountain ranges in the world, never to return to the land of their birth, just so they could bring the Gospel message to the Chinese people.

According to historical findings, many Chinese found Jesus through these Nestorian Christians. If the Chinese, or the rest of the world for that matter, can gain anything from the Nestorians, it is their amazing ability to contextualize the Gospel message by using the style, methods, and even architecture of the people they were trying to reach.

The geological findings of the Nestorian missionaries in China indicate that the Iranian Christian emissaries understood the importance of grafting into the culture, something missionaries today would be wise to learn from.

While we were riding in our taxi outside of Xi'an, we found a little patch of road that curved up the mountain. The hard dirt mounds in the road occasionally scraped along the bottom of the car carriage. Finally we arrived at the Da Qin Pagoda. A Buddhist monk was working outside, in front of the pagoda, in a small communal garden.

The Da Qin Temple does not look any different from the many Buddhist temples I have seen throughout China, and I began to wonder if I had arrived at the right location. Nothing seemed special, but there were a couple of things I had been told to look for that would make it stand out from other Buddhist temples.

The Chinese-style pagoda has a ten-foot-high and five-foot-wide picture of a mountain scene with a clear portrayal of the nativity of Jesus Christ. The nativity scene is supposed to have been done in a way that would be similar to the nativity scenes that are famous in the early churches in Iran. On the next floor, there is a large scene of a tree with a man underneath it, which is not Buddha under a banyan tree but instead is a pictorial version of the story of Jonah.

Martin Palmer made a very convincing argument in his book *The Jesus Sutras* that the pagoda was indeed a Christian structure. Palmer gives four points to back up his evidence:

1. Its name, Da Qin (which means "from the west"), is a reference to the "religion of light" or Nestorian missionaries from the west, meaning west of China.
2. The Da Qin temple points east, but all other Chinese temples face north and south.
3. Several lines of Syriac writing have been found at and around the temple, which would indicate the presence of Nestorians who had fled to the Persian Empire to escape persecution.
4. Pictorial painting of Bible stories can be found on the walls of the pagoda.

When I walked up to the entrance of the pagoda, a small sign was outside, claiming that it had been the site of the Nestorian Christians. When I went through the entrance of the door, I could see a small Buddhist altar that was elaborately decorated with burning incense being offered.

I was struck by the grape fields, which are not a common sight in China, that seemed to be everywhere around the pagoda. At the entrance was a Chinese woman selling honey and wine to a nearby village. The fact that there were vineyards all around the pagoda with Chinese villagers who knew how to make wine was evidence enough for me to prove that the pagoda was planted by missionaries from the Church in the East! Wine was needed for the Lord's Supper and is one of the few things that the Roman Church and Eastern Church shared a passion for.

As I looked down on the villages from the pagoda, I could see an elaborate memorial center being built at the base of the mountain. At the writing of this book, it was not yet completed, but an Iranian Christian church was being constructed with an entrance lined with Iranian pillars that are topped with Zoroastrian bulls, which reflect the religion of the empire where the Nestorian missionaries were sent from. It is truly a strange feeling to be in a small village in China and walk among artifacts from the Iranian royal courts of King Darius.

Only a few meters away from the pagoda was a copy of the Nestorian stone, an exact replica of the one at the museum in Xi'an. In 1623, an ancient stele, or stone tablet, was discovered by the Da Qin Pagoda. The stone tablet stands about eight feet high and is over three feet wide and has ancient Christian text, written in both Chinese and Syriac.

The stone is dated February 4, 781, and was written to commemorate the work of Iranian Christians in China. Much of the Christian work was done by an Iranian missionary named Adam. Adam was obviously a Christian missionary who understood contextualization.

The text of the stele recounts the arrival of Christian missionaries to Xi'an using the Silk Road, the same route used today by the Back to Jerusalem missionaries from China. The first mission team from Iran arrived in Xi'an in AD 635. Immediately they were accepted into the royal Chinese court, and after reading the Word of God, the emperor supported the propagation of the Iranian Christian's teachings.

The Word of God spread from there to many other cities and provinces, and the Iranian Christians were able to establish several monasteries in the land that would one day be ruled by the iron-fisted Mao Zedong.

The stele tells us the history of the work of the missionaries. It was likely paid for by a Chinese Christian, Yi Si, who is described as a highly decorated court official and general in the Chinese army. He was also a Christian teacher, appointed as a bishop, which is yet another example of how the Iranian missionaries were cross-culturally effective.

The stele had a list of over seventy bishops, priests, and monks from the "Luminous Communities of the East."

The Da Qin Temple that used to be a church serves the purposes of a different god today. I felt angry and hurt at first, but then remembered that the day the Da Qin Temple was built, the number of believers in China would have only been a handful. Today, however, there are an estimated 150 million believers.

The Iranian missionaries who built the Da Qin Temple were known for being practically valuable to the community. Adam was obviously useful in linking Iranian culture with Chinese culture through language. Looking at the garden reminded me that the Iranian missionaries were also known to show locals how to grow vegetables and improve food sources by using advanced farming techniques. This flexibility and practicability allowed them into areas that Roman Catholic missionaries could not get into.

I smiled, because this is similar to the Chinese Back to Jerusalem missionaries today who are working in many closed countries around the world showing locals how to improve their food production by implementing advanced farming techniques. Back to Jerusalem missionaries are able to have access to places like South Sudan by taking their farming techniques into the country and showing the locals how to employ the new techniques.

It made me wonder how many of the farming techniques used by the Buddhist farmer today had been taught by the Iranian missionaries.

The Iranian mission model was one of the most successful cross-cultural examples that never has really been told. Even today, few mission organizations have been as successful in the Middle East, Asia, India, and China as the Iranians were. The missionaries in China were not receiving large amounts of financial resources from the Iranian Empire, but they came as humble servants with a wealth of knowledge that could help contribute to the mission community.

***

Xi'an was not the only location in China where evidence was discovered about the successful missionary work from Iran. A cave in western China known as Tun-huang was discovered in 1900 and contained several ancient Christian manuscripts. It was like finding the Dead Sea Scrolls. Among the manuscripts was a painting of a Christian bishop carrying a bishop's rod with a Nestorian cross. One of the intriguing things is that the man is holding up his right hand with the thumb touching the tip of his second finger, as is often seen in Buddhist meditation, and was like the Buddha at the altar at the Da Qin Temple.

The significance of this is the triangular shape of the fingers representing the trinity as well as three fingers pointing to heaven. Earlier paintings of Buddha show his hands open or clasped, but later images have him with his right hand posed in the same manner as the bishop, which raises the question, where did the Buddhist get it from?

The work of the Iranian missionaries played an equally significant part in China's western Xinjiang Province because of the relationship that the missionaries already shared with many of the residents. Missionaries were sent to both Xinjiang and Tibet, but in Xinjiang, among the first settlers of the region, were those who spoke Saka and Tumxuk, both of which are classified as a part of the "Middle Iranian family of languages."

I am all too aware that many scholars and researchers will disagree with my liberal use of the term "Iranian missionary," as many nations, languages, and cultures made up the early Iranian Empire (and still do). This book is not an exhaustive detailed account of history. Rather, its intention is to reveal the significance of the Iranian people in God's Kingdom. It is important that Iran (former Persia) is emphasized so that the reader knows that Iran is not anti-Christian, anti-Jewish, or anti-evangelism. Islam is, and Muslim leaders have worked very hard to erase this important history from the books and the Iranian people's memory.

These Iranian missionaries were given the massive task of taking the Gospel to the Middle Kingdom of China and many other countries around the world. Even today, with an extensive railway system, airports in every major city, and freeways to drive from one end to the other, this is still an unimaginable task. The missionaries from Iran did it at the cost of great personal sacrifice that often ended in martyrdom.

Very little is known about the amazing Christian history of Iran in Iran today, but there are a few traces of it that the enemy has failed to completely erase as we have found in China. Several testimonials of this time period still exist in Iran as well.

A replica of the Nestorian stele is in the Anglican Church of St. Simon in the southern Iranian city of Shiraz, but the doors to that church are usually closed.

The Church of St. Mary in Tabriz, a north-western city of Iran, is considered by some historians to be the second oldest church in the world. As a token of the appreciation for all that the Iranian missionaries did in China, a Chinese princess contributed money to have the Iranian church rebuilt in 642. Her name is engraved on a stone on the church wall to remind the Iranian people what their sacrifice meant to the Chinese people.

Iranian Christians first brought the Gospel message to China, and now it is time for China to return the favor.

6

IRAN AND ISLAM

Today, those of us at Back to Jerusalem see that Iranians are sick of Islam. For the sake of brevity, this chapter will cover only the most obvious aspects of Islam. Some readers might find it offensive and insensitive, but that is not my intention. My intention is to provide a concise analysis with integrity.

Leaving theology aside and without attempting to argue different Koranic texts, the truth is that peace, love, and harmony with other religions do not exist in the history of Islamic countries. Islam demands the absolute and complete subjugation of other religious peoples and is built on a foundation of violence that can be traced throughout history.

A nation's religion will shape the culture of the people. Unfortunately, that has been the case in Iran. An American or European arriving in Iran for the first time may not be able to articulate the differences they see and feel right away, but after only a short time of exposure, it will be apparent that something is very different.

The religion of Islam puts very little value on the individual and individual justice. Justice only exists for the male Muslim, and that aspect is ever-present in Iran. Women, children, and non-Muslim males are dispensable.

Jesus' teachings shaped Western culture in the same way that Middle Eastern culture has been shaped by Muhammad's. Justice for individuals, especially the weakest and least desirable, is of utmost importance for those who follow Jesus.

Christianity gave birth to new ideas of forgiveness, compassion, and love.

Muhammad's teaching, however, brought different ideas, ideas of subjugation, submission, and retribution. The vengeful invasion of Mecca after Muhammad's exile to Medina in the seventh century shaped the way Islamic victors treated the Iranians when they conquered Iran. Even today, more than a thousand years since the invasion of the Islamic armies from Arabia, it is not easy for Iranians to accept their defeat. And because so much of Islam is intertwined with Arabic culture and vice versa, the Iranians are constantly reminded of that defeat.

Islamic prayers, for instance, can only be offered in the Arabic language. Iranians are forced to read and write with Arabic characters. Often Iranian resentment from the demands of Islam spill over in the form of negative sentiments toward Arabs. I have seen it happen.

During one of my first trips to Iran, I talked to an Iranian named Farad about the difference between Arabs and Persians. He informed me quickly and firmly that it could be considered offensive to refer to an Iranian as an Arab. "Iranians have culture," he said, as if to suggest that Arabs do not. "Islam was forced upon us," he continued. "We never chose it. Persians were superior to the Arabs who invaded Iran in almost every way except for military ferocity."

His words about the Arabic people seem harsh, but they reflect the feelings of many Iranians. Maybe it is these sentiments that set the Iranians apart from the rest of the Middle East. Iranians are the Islamic rebels. In the region of the Persian Gulf, it is no doubt that they are the ones always pushing the limits of Islam.

The dark history of Iran's Islamic beginnings are hidden in history, but today the chains that bind them are being broken by some of the young people, and most of them are choosing the freedom of Jesus Christ. This newfound freedom is being met by violence, imprisonment, and executions.

No matter how hard they fight, though, Islam is still the dominant religion in Iran, but they cannot be blamed for that, any more than a slave can be blamed for being a slave. When Muslim conquerors came to Iran, they had a strong policy of conversion by the sword. They collected taxes from non-Muslims and took the wives and daughters of the conquered as their concubines.

This chapter of history is dark and hideous. It is important to understand the true history of Iran to understand the current situation today.

Just prior to Islam in the early seventh century, Iran was having problems with social unrest. The Iranians were not as warm and welcoming toward the Christians as they once were, and Christians were being persecuted and taxed because of the war with the Romans. Iranians did not see their backward, migrant Arab neighbors as a big threat. After all, how could a world-class super power be defeated by nomads?

The Iranians and their relaxed attitude toward their neighbors did not take into account how unhappy the majority of the population was with the leadership in Iran, including the Christians. There were many hopes, even among the Christians, that the Muslim invaders would give more freedom than the Iranian rulers. Islam was new, and not much was known about it, but rumors spread rapidly that it was a religion that made all men equal.

The mighty Iranian empire was conquered by Muslim Arabs in 644. The Iranian capital city was completely destroyed by the invading army. Iranian wealth was looted by the invading Arabs, who immediately indulged their every pleasure. Local allies were rewarded, and opposition was squashed. Iranians were eventually forced to abandon even their own written language and accept the Arabic script.

Many of the Iranians, including the Christians who welcomed the Muslim invaders, were used to seeing magnanimous armies and had hoped for a King Cyrus–type of victor. That is not what occurred. Free men were turned into slaves, and when the slaves were not enough, a country that previously did not practice slavery imported thousands of African slaves to carry out laborious work.

Buddhists were slaughtered, and their places of worship were completely destroyed. The dominant religion of Zoroastrianism soon followed a similar fate. The Christians and Jews were able to escape the brunt of the persecution, although not completely, because Muslims had "some" respect for people of the "book." Unfortunately for the Islamic victors, the Christians were very well educated and were needed as bankers, accountants, teachers, doctors, etc.

Soon, Christians were forced to wear clothing that differentiated them from the Muslims. The newly established Rashidun Caliphate designated the Church of the East as an official dhimmi minority group, meaning that they were now subjected to pay jizyah to the Islamic rulers. The Christians in Iran were viewed with extreme mistrust and were not allowed to ride on horseback beside a Muslim who was walking on foot. They were not allowed to hold office or carry weapons.

Mass conversions to Christianity began to take place because of the violence, injustice, and economic burdens brought on by Islam.

Christians were restricted within the caliphate, but they were also given a degree of protection in the same manner that mobs protect those who pay bribes. After the Muslims secured control of Iran and the majority of Iranians became Muslims, there was a constant on-again, off-again love affair with the Christians. Some years they would show favor and mercy to the Christians, and other years were absolutely frightening in the reign of terror. There were periods of persecution and acceptance.

Just as Islam came from Arabia to Iran, so too did the nomadic traditions. Even for the Islamic nations of Somalia, Malaysia, Pakistan, and Maldives, all of which are not Arabic, to properly follow Islam meant, to some extent, taking on the identity of nomadic Arabs.

The Persians were not any different. For them to be followers of Islam, they had to partially take on the identity of Arabs. As a result, some of the grand history and identity of the Iranian achievements were lost to Arab history.

In practice, this means that as orthodox Islamic influence increases, the growth and development of business, education, science, and medicine all suffer decrease. This idea is not acceptable in politically correct circles, but history is a patient teacher.

When the chains of Islam are loosened and true Christianity is given liberty and freedom, national and cultural identity flourish and there is progress and development in the fields of business, education, science, and medicine. Historically, wherever Islamic orthodoxy is embraced, advancement, growth, and freedom are stifled.

This is in direct conflict with many liberal educational institutions today that promote the history of Islam as being enlightened. A careful study will show that any advancement in medicine, astronomy, math, or business recorded in Islamic history was either a result of a period of unorthodox liberal Islamic practice or the residual impact of the conquered.

In any dialogue, Iranian Muslim scholars rightly point out the plethora of atrocities Muslims have historically suffered at the hands of Christians. The difference is non-Christians who have suffered at the hands of Christians are always the result of unorthodox Christianity. By definition, an orthodox Christian, or someone who is a true follower of Jesus Christ, adheres to the teachings on love, mercy, forgiveness, and self-sacrifice. Followers of Jesus Christ, where the term *Christian* is derived, do not kill, force conversions, or physically harm the non-believer. Jesus' words and teachings were clear and leave very little room for misinterpretation.

Christians are commanded to love their enemies and forgive their transgressors.

With Islam, this is not the case.

Muhammad had two sides to him. One is often referred to as

the pre-Medina era and the other is the post-Medina era, and it is these two eras that make up the writings in the Koran. During the pre-Medina, or the period when Muhammad was forced to leave Mecca, Muhammad wanted to gain a following and acceptance among the Christians and the Jews, so he wrote and taught about peace and love between his new revelation, the Christians, and the Jews. However, after he was banished from Mecca, Muhammad did not deal with rejection well. He scorned the existence of the Christians and Jews who rejected him. It led to the writings promoting bloodshed, war, and ruthless violence.

Jesus' followers have no examples of Jesus waging war, committing theft, or raping. In Muhammad, Muslims have many examples of Muhammad robbing caravans, killing merchants and non-combatants, and even raping pre-adolescent children.

If this is not clearly understood, then it is impossible to understand what Islam has done to the Iranian people and her culture.

When the Mongols first invaded Iran, they had a great distrust of the followers of Islam. Prior to that, they did find a level of honesty among the Christians of the Nestorian missions they had encountered in Central Asia and had appointed them to high offices.

In 1282, one Mongol ruler decreed that all government clerks should either be Christian or Jewish.

The favor that the Christians experienced under Mongol rule was short-lived when the Mongols concluded that it was better to side with the Islamic masses in the newly occupied Iran.

The Shi'ite faith became the state religion of Iran during the reign of Shah Isma'il Safavi who was from present-day Azerbaijan. During this time, a renaissance of Islam took place in Iran that changed the country forever.

Today in Iran, Shi'a Muslims have a different way of praying than Sunnis, and this is a way that the two can be visibly identified: Sunnis fold their arms during their prayer, but Shi'ites keep their arms loose. The Shi'ites keep a piece of clay from Karbala in front of them and will place their foreheads on it as they lean forward prostrated in prayer.

Both Shi'ites and Sunnis teach many of the same doctrines, and both place the highest value on the Five Pillars of Faith, including the pilgrimage to Mecca. One of the major differences between the two groups is not doctrinal. Instead, the main difference is about leadership and who should lead the Islamic community.

When reflecting on the history of Islam in Iran, the armies of political correctness will either compare this time period to some period of Christian cruelty or claim that the events in ancient history are not a true representation of real Islam.

To understand what the Iranians have had to deal with, it is important to at least read a few of the hundreds of Koranic and Hadith verses that speak of warfare, violence, killing, and bloodshed.

Since the September 11, 2001, attacks in the United States, many Christian countries in Europe and North America have become more alert and have educated themselves about the large section of Islamic teaching regarding Jihad. As a result, many Muslims have tried to change the meaning of *Jihad* and explain it away.

However, it is hard to reframe Koranic teachings such as, "But when the forbidden months are past, then fight and slay the Pagans wherever you find them and seize them, beleaguer them, and lie in wait for them in every stratagem of war."

Jihad is the crux of the Muslim faith and is taught as the duty of every Muslim believer.

In the parts of Iran where Christianity had once been the faith of the majority, they are now predominately Muslim. This happened by force. Like the black robes of the Iranian leaders today, Islam drapes over a grand monument hiding the rich history, poetry, fascinating culture, and academic conquests of the Iranian people.

Today, many Iranians want to be free from Islam.

7

IRAN WAITING ON A SAVIOR

When it comes to keeping Iranians from the teachings of Jesus, the cards are stacked against the Islamic leaders. If you would like to know why the leaders have to rule the Iranian people with an iron fist, this chapter explains why.

Iran has always seemed mysterious to the foreign traveler. There is a spiritual awareness in Iran that seems less dogmatic than the Arabs and much more mystical. The ideas of flying carpets, snake charmers, and Aladdin (a Middle Eastern tale that takes place in China, not the Middle East) have enchanted the minds of foreigners for generations. These icons might be considered to be misleadingly stereotypical, but they do capture the mysticism and enchanted beauty that exists in ancient Iran.

The word *paradise* is a word that comes from the Persian language. Iran has seemed like a paradise for some, but it's also been hell on earth for many.

Even in Iran's submission to Islam, they are still rebellious. They are the only country in the world to follow Shia Islam as a national religion. It appears they are out to spite the rest of the Sunni world. Although the Iranians might have to accept Islam, they accept it on their own terms.

This doctrinal difference of Shia Islam might seem like any other brand of Islam, but compared to other Muslim nations, it provides many opportunities for Christianity to grow. Iranian Islam makes followers especially open to the truth of God's Word.

Shia Islam in itself is not special, but what it represents in Iran is an amazing door opener for the Gospel message.

One of the things that makes the Iranians open to the Gospel is the close correlation between their belief in Shia Islam and Jesus Christ. Many will be repulsed by the idea that there is a connection between anything Islam and Jesus, but it is there for those who search.

At first glance, many people may view Shia Islam as an aspect of Islam much like Christianity has many denominations. However, this is where one must be careful. The divisions that exist in Christianity between the Catholic, Eastern Orthodox, and Protestant churches are a result of division among believers years after the resurrection of Christ. The division between Shia and Sunnis happened during the establishment of the religion.

It is not just Shia Islam but specifically the Iranian practice of Shia Islam that is of interest to the Christian missionaries coming from China. One out of every five Muslims are Shia, and almost 40 percent of all Muslims in the Middle East are Shia. The division between Sunni and Shia is the largest and oldest in all of Islam.

The religion of Islam was established by Muhammad in the seventh century AD. In 622, he set up the first Islamic state, a theocracy in Medina, a city in Saudi Arabia. There are two branches of the religion he started: Sunni and Shi'ite (also known as Shia). The difference between the two largest Muslim groups originated with a controversy over who got to take power after the Prophet Muhammad's death in 632 AD. The Sunni branch believes the first four caliphs—Muhammad's successors—rightfully took his place as the leaders of Islam. They recognize the heirs of the four caliphs as legitimate rulers. These heirs held power continuously in the Arab world until the break-up of the Ottoman Empire following the end of the First World War.

Shi'ites, in contrast, believe only the heirs of the fourth caliph, Ali, are the legitimate successors of Muhammad. In 931, the Twelfth Imam disappeared. This was an impacting event in the history of Shi'ite Muslims who are concentrated in Iran, Iraq, and

Lebanon and who believe they suffered the loss of divinely guided political leadership at the time of the Imam's disappearance. Not until the ascendancy of Iran's Ayatollah Ruhollah Khomeini in 1978 did they believe they had once again begun to live under the authority of a legitimate religious figure. Al-Qaeda, until May 2011 ruled by Osama bin Laden, is a Sunni Muslim terrorist organization. The Lebanese terrorist organization Hezbollah is a Shi'ite-backed group. Iran is Shi'ite. The two factions are in most cases bitterly opposed to each other. Both are avowed enemies to Israel and the West.

When Muhammad, the founder of Islam, died in the early seventh century, he left behind not only a religion but an empire. He appointed his cousin, Ali, to be his successor. Although Ali was his first cousin, he married Muhammad's daughter, which also made him his son-in-law.

Although it is believed that all of Muhammad's teachings are directly from God and should be adhered to when it comes to choosing a successor, many Muslims felt that the successor should be selected by a team of elders.

To put it simply, Shias believe that God selected Muhammad as his prophet and that God also appointed his successors. Sunnis believe that God was wise in his selection of the prophet, but that man should be entrusted with electing the new leader.

After Muhammad's death, the Sunnis chose Abu Bakr as the next caliph, who was technically Muhammad's father-in-law. Ali, Muhammad's son-in-law, was later chosen as the fourth caliph after the death of Abu Bakr's successor.

Ali and Fatimah were the only ones who were able to give Muhammad descendants, and one of their children, Hussein, married the daughter of the last emperor of Iran prior to the spread of Islam.

Hussein, the Prophet Muhammad's grandson and husband to an Iranian princess, rose up against a superior Islam force and was martyred. This killing is the most significant in Shia Islam and created a violent divide between Sunni and Shia.

Hussein's martyrdom brought about a messianic doctrine in Islam that believes a messiah-like figure will return to restore world order. Hussein was revered as an Imam to the Iranians, and his marriage to the last princess of Iran made him even more endearing to the Iranian people.

It is here that there is a wide door open to the Iranian Muslims. Sunni Muslims are not able to accept that Jesus, or Isa as He is known in Islam, died on a cross. Muslims believe that it is not possible for a prophet to be crucified because they think God would not allow it. Muslims believe that Jesus was a prophet, that He was born of a virgin Mary, that He performed miracles, and in the Koran, He is actually referred to as Jesus Christ or Messiah.

They believe that Jesus was a Muslim and was miraculously saved prior to being crucified and therefore never died on the cross.

Shia Muslims hold to a different set of beliefs. The Shias do not have any problem understanding the idea of sacrifice for the greater good because they have Hussein as their example. Hussein's martyrdom is remembered every year in Iran. Writing in blood-like red can be seen on cars, and even random water fountains in Iran will spew out water with red dye to observe his death.

Sometimes rituals involving self-flagellation are also practiced to commemorate the pain and suffering of the Prophet Hussein.

Because of their belief about the death of Hussein, Iranian Shi'ite Muslims often more quickly identify with the sacrifice of Jesus on the cross than Sunni Muslims. Again, this is only a bridge for sharing the Gospel message. However, it is not a small one.

Another doorway into sharing Christianity can be found in the celebration of Hussein's martyrdom as a day that Shia Muslims believe they can be forgiven of their sins. This atonement based not on works but on the sacrifice of someone sent by God is another important bridge between Islam and Christianity.

This event, known as Ashura, is remembered with a sober heart much in the way that Easter is remembered by Christians. Just as

Christians make pilgrimages to Calvary where Jesus was crucified, Shia Muslims go to the place where Hussein was martyred. Some believe Hussein can even mediate between God and man for the sins of man. Shia Muslims in Iran believe that evil was defeated by Hussein, but there will be a messianic figure who will return one day, the Mahdi, and his return will coincide with the second coming of Jesus Christ. The Mahdi will be the Twelfth Imam and will come to restore order, justice, and truth. The return of the Mahdi is absolutely central to the Iranian belief in Islam and could be useful for connecting with the Muslims in Iran.

This does not mean that Christians use Islam to teach Muslims about the truth of Jesus Christ. This simply means that Shia Islam presents many bridges to connect an unbeliever with the idea of Jesus' teachings and could help Shia Muslims understand concepts that Christ taught. Just as Jesus used parables to teach His disciples about God, a Chinese missionary is able to use Shia teachings to explain concepts that are found in the Bible. The bridges are so numerous and present so many opportunities that it is not possible to cover them all in this chapter, but here's a look at a few:

- In Shia Islam, a paraclete, or a comforter, is sent to guide believers on the path of truth, just as the Holy Spirit is sent to be a comforter to followers of Jesus.
- Shia Islam teaches that there will be an anti-Christ-like figure who will be connected to forehead markings, similar to what is taught in Revelation 14:9.
- There is a unique devotion toward Fatimah, the holy mother of the martyred prophet Hussein (as well as the mother-in-law of the last Iranian princess), which could relate to understanding Jesus' mother, Mary.

In addition to the beliefs of Shia Islam, there is also the aforementioned deeply rooted background of Zoroastrianism, the early religion of Iran. Even after all the efforts to completely erase any and all ideas of Christianity from the history and culture of the

Iranian people, they are still there. The similarities, links, and bridges are like stubborn stains that cannot be removed from the walls of Iran's history.

In Iran's secret corners, one will also find that Iran is not just Shia with historical traces of Zoroastrianism, but there are many Iranians who are also Sufi. Sufism is a strong blend of Islam with the mysticism of Zoroastrianism, and it is extremely important for Christians who work in Iran or who pray for Iran to understand the practices of Sufis.

Sufism is not supported by the Iranian government, but Iran is home to the largest number of Sufis in the world. Sufi followers in Iran talk about experiencing God in ways that some Muslims find blasphemous.

Sufism is a better fit for many Iranians because of the music, dancing, lyrical chanting, and mysticism involved. It is a very charismatic expression of Islam that is not embraced by the orthodox clergy. In short, Sufism is a personal experience of God that is subjective rather than objective. It is a spiritual journey of supernatural experiences where Allah is more personal than in orthodox Islam. Like Christians, Sufis believe that God can speak directly to man without mediation.

For a Sufi, Allah lives in the hearts of his followers and can guide them to truth, and it is this kind of spiritual element that already exists in Iran that has played a major factor in the growth of the Christian church in Iran.

Mansur al-Hallaj, an Iranian who lived in the tenth century, was one of the most well-known Sufis who was martyred after seemingly revealing a lot about the love of Jesus Christ. From his teachings, many Muslim accusers thought that he was a crypto-Christian, one who was actually a Christian trying to disguise himself as a Muslim.

Mansur taught that it was possible God could be incarnate and could be one with man. He was a revolutionary writer who stirred the spirits of many Muslim followers. Again, this chapter is not advocating that Shia Islam or Sufism are Christian in their doctrines or teachings, but only that bridges exist to reach those who are in darkness.

The Gospel message will not just accidentally appear in Iran one day and slip into the Iranian culture again undetected. Missionaries, Bibles, and Christian resources must be sent without delay. The objective of the missionaries in Iran is clear, but they are not starting from scratch. God has clearly provided a unique way for missionaries to connect.

Chinese Back to Jerusalem missionaries believe that the Gospel message has been woven into the fabric of the very heart of the Iranian people. They are searching for the "lover of their souls." If they search for Him, they will find Him, and the enemy cannot stop it. The enemy knows that he cannot stop it, so he has used Islam to redirect their passion. The web of lies that the enemy has weaved to cover up the grand history of the Iranian people is becoming undone.

The Gospel message is not foreign to Iran but is central to it. Jehovah is in Iranian culture and history. He is in their hearts and souls. Like gravity, it will take a lot of power to continue fighting the pull of His love. One day they will give up the fight and find rest in His arms.

When this happens, when the lies of Islam are exposed and the evil and torture that the people have needlessly faced for generations have reached an end, there will be a high price to pay for the Muslim leaders. The Muslim clerics have every incentive to prevent the truth from ever being revealed to their countrymen, because they will be the ones held responsible. They will fight with every drop of blood and energy they can muster, knowing that their survival depends on the continuing oppression of the masses.

8
REVOLUTION COMING

You might have heard the story of the Islamic Revolution in Iran, but you have most likely never heard it told like it will be in this chapter. Failing to understand what lead to the revolution will result in an inability to understand Iran today.

Everything that defines Iran today is overshadowed by the revolution. No one could have foreseen how the drastic changes that were imposed after 1979 would change the course of history of Iran forever.

The revolution did not come without popular support. The people asked for it. Many of them even begged for it, although today most of them are experiencing buyer's remorse.

It was similar to the grassroots excitement when Communism marched into town in China. The ideas of justice for the poor, equality for the downtrodden, and a better economy for all were attractive to the citizenry. But October 1, 1949, was a day that changed China. Students were marching through the streets, factory union leaders were shouting victoriously, and peasant farmers were singing with joy. Those shouts of victory were soon drowned out by the cries of mothers and fathers as family, friends, and neighbors began to be systematically killed for the "cause." Temples were destroyed, books were burned, laws were changed, and the young people found themselves in one of the darkest moments in history, not just for China, but for mankind.

Thirty years later, Iran matched China in their political passion. Young people were marching through the streets. Like the Reds, they demanded change. They demanded the overthrow of the leaders. They demanded a revolution.

It is important to know that Iranians were not necessarily supporting Islam when they supported the revolution. They were looking for equality, justice, and equal opportunity, and the Muslim clergy played off of those desires and tried to represent the change that the people wanted.

Just as the revolution in China was built on the idealism of youth, the Muslim leadership was able to tap into the zeal of the university students and turn them against their government. They convinced the Iranians that the West had taken away the identity of Iran and that Iran needed to go back to their Shia roots. The people were persuaded.

Iran was not always the way it is today. Before 1979, Iran's relationship with the United States was considered stable and strong.

The revolution in 1979 did not just spontaneously happen. There were external factors that contributed to the perfect storm.

Reza Shah came to power in Iran in 1925. He was a dictator when being a dictator was an international fad. His rise was similar to the likes of Mussolini, Hitler, and Mao Zedong.

When Reza became shah (or king), he did not think well of Islam. Communism was sweeping the world stage, but Reza Shah decided to take a different path. Since he was not fond of the Soviet communists, he led Iranians back to their own culture. It was an Iranian cultural revival with a secular twist.

Reza Shah knew that Iranians thought of themselves as superior to the Arabs, and he decided to play off of their pride. He reminded the people of their historical achievements in a way that completely isolated and excluded Islam.

Just as Mao built roads and railroads, Reza also built bridges, roads, and railroads all across the country.

Mao brought China together after it had been ravaged by the Japanese. Reza Shah brought Iran together after a series of humiliating defeats and planned to make it great again.

Mao and Reza both created centralized systems for the military, education, domestic transport infrastructure, taxing and finances, as well as manufacturing.

There is also an uncanny resemblance between Mao and Reza in the way they both were so determined to attack religion. Before Mao burned Bibles, Reza Shah banned turbans and beards for men and banned women from wearing the traditional Islamic covering. Anyone caught wearing these items could be stopped and humiliated by the police. They also risked having their clothing removed.

Reza inflicted punishment on the faithful Muslims who felt obligated to keep Islamic customs. He shut down religious schools and opened up state ones. He founded the University of Tehran. He opened a medical school and allowed women to attend. Under his rule, all restaurants, theaters, and hotels had to accept women as equal customers. In essence, he declared war on Islam in Iran.

***

When Adolph Hitler came to power in Germany in 1933, Reza started a relationship between Berlin and Tehran that would lead to a very odd alliance.

The Shah was captivated by the German leader. The Iranian leader began to identify strongly with the Third Reich. So strong was his identification with Nazi ideology that in less than two years, the Shah announced that he was changing the name of his country from Persia to Iran.

The term *Persia* originated from the Greeks, who called themselves Iranians, which means "land of the Aryans." Iran was officially adopted as the new name of the country. The land of the Aryan race was now official.

Many elites and intellectuals in Iran encouraged the idea of Aryan superiority. Germany became the number one trading partner of Iran, and the obsession with racial superiority dominated the national dialogue.

Reza Shah once wrote,

> *Germany was our age-old and natural ally. Love of Germany was synonymous with love for Iran. The sound of German officers' footsteps was heard on the shores of the Nile. Swastika flags were flying from the outskirts of Moscow to the peaks of the Caucasus Mountains. Iranian patriots eagerly awaited the arrival of their old allies. My friend and I would spin tales about grandeur of the superior race. We consider Germany the chosen representative of this race in Europe and Iran its representative in Asia. The right to life and role was ours. Others had not choice, but submission and slavery.*

Germany advocated the common Aryan ancestry of the two nations, and the Reich issued a special decree in 1936 exempting Iranians from the restrictions of the Nuremberg Race Laws on the grounds that the Iranians were pure-blooded Aryans.

Nazi Gestapo agents were sent to Iran, and Iran became the focus of Germany's Middle East efforts during World War II. To keep up the ruse and pat each other on the back, Nazi Germany provided Iran with a "German Scientific Library," which contained over 7,500 books to show the Iranian readers the kinship between the National Socialist Reich and the Aryan culture of Iran.

The day that Iran officially changed their name will long be remembered by the citizens. For many, the name *Iran* will forever remind them of the connection that they had with Nazi Germany.

Because of the alliance with Germany, the British and Russians eventually invaded Iran. They were met with little resistance from the Iranian army, and Reza Shah was removed from power. He fled to South Africa, where he eventually died.

His son, Muhammad Reza, was named Shah in 1941. It seems the power of the British and Russian military to overpower the Iranian Army did not affect the new Shah's self-image in the least. After assuming power, Mohammad Reza Shah bequeathed upon himself many titles—Emperor, Light of the Aryans, and Head of the Warriors, just to name a few. In 1967, he chose to accept the title of King of Kings; he felt that "he did not deserve it" until then. The coronation ceremony for the "King of Kings" was opulent, as coronation ceremonies for the King of Kings often are.

Video footage was broadcast all around the world of a horse and carriage accompanied by servants and soldiers dressed in European-style uniforms.

The images of wealth and royalty on screen did not impress the common people of Iran. During that time, many Iranians were living in poverty and were struggling to survive. That was not the best time for the leader to brag about opulent riches.

In many ways, the new young Shah was like a cat with nine lives. He survived several assassination attempts and coups. One assassination attempt was carried out by a man who was standing barely ten feet from the Shah, fired five shots at him, and somehow managed to miss with every bullet except for one that merely grazed the Shah.

A former KGB agent who had defected told a story of a bomb that was connected to a TV remote control that was placed in a Volkswagen Beetle and was strategically placed to kill the Shah, but it failed to detonate.

Upon learning of the British MI6, Russian KGB, and the American CIA, the Shah decided to create a secret service of his own. In the 1960s, the Shah installed one of the most elite secret services in the Middle East called SAVAK. The SAVAK was ruthless and without mercy and went after the Shah's political opponents with a vengeance. According to human rights watch dogs, the SAVAK secret police were one of the most cruel human rights abusers on the planet.

The Shah was known to be extravagant, throwing parties and living in posh conditions while the rest of the country suffered. When the people grumbled about his opulence or posed a threat, they were severely punished. The Shah defended his actions by saying, "When the Iranians learn to behave like Swedes, I will behave like the King of Sweden." History has shown he was an egocentric leader who lost touch with his people.

His relationship with the Western world continued to grow stronger, and his relationship with the Islamic clerics grew further apart. Polygamy and child marriages were outlawed, women were allowed to hold almost any job, including that of a judge or minister, and non-Muslims such as Jews and Christians were able to live without fear of government persecution based on religion. Overall, though, it seemed that the policies and Westernization were both helping and hurting the people at the lowest levels in Iran. The lives of the common Iranians seemed to be getting better in some ways, but at a cost that many citizens were not willing or able to live with.

The Shah always felt that he was good to the people of Iran and acted in their best interest as their king. But he did not really have a good understanding of the root of their dissatisfaction. Surrounding himself with consultants and advisors who did not paint him a real picture of how his people felt about him or about the status of his country was also a weakness of his leadership.

Strangely, even though there seemed to be more freedom for Christians in Iran prior to the 1979 Revolution, the number of Christians remained relatively low. The Iranians did not seem to be interested in Christianity.

After almost forty years of rule, the people felt that the Shah had been in power long enough. The King of Kings in Iran had taken for granted the people he ruled over. The divide between him and the common Iranian on the street was too wide. They wanted a leader they could support. They were ripe for a revolution.

Now, more than thirty-five years since the revolution, many in Iran look back on the days of the Shah as the good old days. The hardships that were experienced under the Shah in the 1970s seem like a day at Disneyland compared to what they are experiencing today. Many of the supporters of the revolution long to be able to turn back history. Unfortunately, that is not an option.

As the days of the Shah's reign were coming to a close, Satan was preparing the heart of a man who would promise to be the savior of the Iranian people, but he would only lead them deeper into slavery and darkness. Islamic cleric Khomeini painted a picture of refuge with his Islamic teachings, and the masses were convinced. However, his teachings were among some of the darkest in the world. In the next chapter, we will look at what Khomeini said and wrote to get a better picture of the man who would next rule Iran.

9

THE REVOLUTION

The story of the revolution reveals a lot about Ayatollah Ruhollah Khomeini. Khomeini is Iran today. He is the embodiment of the country. The country and the man are not easy to separate; he is the central figure in the shaping of Iran in the twenty-first century. Rarely has a country been so absolutely molded by one person as Iran has by Khomeini. A dictator is a dangerous thing, but a dictator with Allah on his side is absolutely disastrous on a cosmic scale. The revolution that Khomeini led might have been one of the largest open demonstrations in history in terms of the sheer number of people who turned out. But instead of focusing on the revolution, this chapter will focus more on the leader of the Revolution. Much more can be understood about the revolution and Iran today by studying Khomeini and what he said and wrote.

***

The Shah's efforts to secularize Iran, privately consume a large portion of the country's oil revenue windfall, and beat the citizenry into compliance was not without backlash. His face was everywhere. The Shah's image was on documents, money, at the beginning of every movie played in Iranian theaters, on billboards, and on posters. These images of the Shah were meant to remind the people of his greatness, but once the Muslim clerics were able to paint him as an evil puppet of the American government and an enemy of Allah, every picture of the Shah only reminded the people of the root cause of their problems.

71

In 1976, three years prior to the Revolution, the Shah even changed the calendar to begin on the day that King Cyrus marched into Babylon instead of the day that the Prophet Muhammad marched from Medina to Mecca. This change worked out perfectly, with the Shah's reign starting in 2500, an auspicious number in Persian culture, thus giving him good luck.

When the Shah switched the calendar, it was an affront to Iran's Muslim community. Few were more indignant than Ruhollah Khomeini, the future Ayatollah.

Most books and historians like to focus on what happened during the Revolution, but for our purposes, it is much more important to understand the leader of the Revolution. What happened during the Revolution is merely a byproduct.

"Ayatollah is like a high priest or top religious leader," one of the Tehran locals explained to me as we stared at a poster of the top Ayatollah. "Most people associate it with the two supreme leaders of Iran, but that is not true. It is more of a title for an Islamic teacher. However, because of the power that the religious leaders now have in Iran, the term 'Ayatollah' is interchangeable with 'supreme leader.'" The Iranian took a deep breath wanting to say more but very noticeably exercised restraint and didn't say anything else.

Ruhollah Khomeini was born Ruhollah Mousavi, which means "inspired of God." He was from the Iranian town of Khomein, so he adopted the name of his home town when he took the name he is known by today: Ruhollah Khomeini. The fact that his name was not his real name has contributed greatly to conspiracy theories that Khomeini was actually a secret CIA agent, which the Shah believed until the day he died.

Khomeini saw the Shah of Iran as an enemy to the Islamic way of life. When the Shah declared the open secularization of Iran, Khomeini was determined to do something about it. In 1963, a protest against the Shah broke out. More than 100,000 people marched in front of the Shah's palace and shouted, "Death to the dictator, death to the dictator! God save you, Khomeini! Death to the blood thirsty enemy!"

Two days after the protests, a group of secret commandos working for the Shah waited in the dark outside of Khomeini's home. They knew that they could not conduct the raid during the day because it would spark even more of an outcry. In the wee hours of the morning, the signal was given to bust into Khomeini's home in Qom and take him to the maximum security prison in Tehran.

The arrest led to violent protests and attacks on police stations throughout Iran. Martial law was declared, and the country was on the brink of anarchy.

The Shah was forced to release Khomeini. Khomeini was prevented from making any more public speeches, but it was too late. His following had grown to an astronomical size, and his supporters were radical. Instead of being strictly political, Khomeini had taught a radical version of Islam. He used the Koran to inspire his followers with the teachings of Muhammad. A leader was born.

His charismatic personality and absolute devotion to the Koran was a winning formula for developing a radical following among the Iranian people. Day after day, Khomeini taught the people how the Shah was being controlled by the Americans and Jews. Mickey Mouse was one of the primary examples. Most people do not know it, but Walt Disney was recruited by the US government as an agent for the FBI to use his communication medium to counter a Communist agenda. Iran was no exception. Images of Mickey Mouse were often used in Iran to promote anti-Communist ideas. Although this might have helped the Iranians to hold off the evils of Communism, it did validate Khomeini's teachings of US control and involvement in Iran.

When the Shah made a deal with the United States that the American government could ask for anyone in Iran to be released from prison at any time, for any reason, this again undermined the

Iranian people and added fuel to the fire. For this concession, the Shah's Iran was given a huge $200 million grant to supply their military with modern arms.

After the agreement with the Americans, Khomeini declared, "They have sold our independence!" For his aggressive speech, he was sent out of Iran. The followers of Khomeini were infuriated that their leader could be kicked out of his own country. They blamed it squarely on the influence from the United States. People found it absurd that an Iranian who grew up and lived in Iran could just be kicked out of his own country at the snap of the fingers of the Americans. The Shah looked like a mere puppet, and Khomeini shone like a hero. Even though he was forced to find refuge in Iraq, his influence over Iranian politics continued to grow.

Khomeini was one of the first people to employ the power of cutting-edge technology to spread religious messages. In fact, his methods are being used on the mission field today. The religious icon was not allowed to set foot in Iran, but from Iraq, he preached message after message, and his team recorded the messages on cassette tapes. Cassette tapes were swapped in an underground network of exchanges. Enthusiastic supporters would smuggle cassette tapes into Iran and distribute them all over the country. As the number of supporters grew, the need for more cassette tapes also grew. Although he could not broadcast a TV program into the country, Khomeini kept the growing number of supporters fed with new messages on cassette tapes.

When I first arrived in China in the '90s, I was a part of the same strategy, but it was for a different purpose. I worked with a legendary missionary from Finland named Teacher Zhao. Teacher Zhao, or Zhao Laoshi, is not well known because all his work was done in secret to support the underground church in China.

In the late '90s, Zhao worked together with the underground church to create one of the first systematic Bible teachings in China to be made by the underground house church. Seminary teaching and Bible study courses were widely available from America and Europe and could have easily been translated into Mandarin, but Zhao worked to create one of the first Bible teaching courses that were taught by the leaders of the underground house church for the members of the underground house church.

It was a massive program made up of hundreds of hours of teachings that were recorded on DAT (Digital Audio Tapes) and re-recorded onto cassette tapes. Together, we carried cassette duplicator machines into China across the Shenzhen border from an office out of Aberdeen, Hong Kong. The cassette duplicators were sent all around the country to set up distribution centers, and just like that, the first indigenous underground Chinese cassette Bible school was born.

Khomeini's supporters did very much the same thing with his teachings throughout Iran with cassette teachings. Even today, Back to Jerusalem missionaries are working with the Iranian underground church to do something very similar. However, instead of using cassettes, it is with modern technology.

The regime in Iran is all too aware of the impact of this kind of distribution and has worked very hard to keep it from happening. Today, it is illegal to circumvent censorship and do what Khomeini did. However, the techniques that Khomeini used are coming back to haunt the regime that inherited their leadership from him, because those same techniques are being used by the Back to Jerusalem missionaries and others to spread the message of the Gospel.

***

While in exile, Khomeini wrote about the rule of Shia Islam as a government model, and his writings also made it into Iran through the underground distribution network. Some of these writings shed light on one of the darkest people in the twenty-first century. They give us a glimpse of how his mind worked and reveal how much control he intended to exert on the people of

Iran. Some of these teachings made it into an infamous book called *The Little Green Book*. That is not what he called it. Khomeini originally published the book in Arabic. In Farsi, the book is called *Tahrirolvasyleh*.

Mao Zedong also wrote a similar book a few years earlier that was required reading for every person living in China, and like *The Little Green Book*, it was intended to control the thoughts of the people. That book was called *Mao's Little Red Book* and became the most printed book in history.

The Little Green Book touched on everything pertaining to life such as food, taxes, dealing with criminals, paying fines, and relationships. The breadth and depth of control reveals how intrusive the Khomeini aspired to be.

The Little Green Book contained the essentials for any good Shia Muslim. It made it clear that men should be put to death for turning from Islam and women should be imprisoned. "The child of a Muslim or that of an apostate, whether national or innate, is considered Muslim before the father's apostasy, and therefore, if the child reached puberty and chose infidelity he will be asked to repent (and return to Islam), else he should be executed."[1]

The book has been translated, but the translations are hard to decipher because of the confusing Arabic. The Farsi translation is also a challenge. The book shows one of the rare looks into the dark side of Khomeini, and there is a reason why most people have not heard of it. After reading it, it is clear why Iranians wanted to keep the book a secret. Here are sixteen highlights to give examples of the fatwas laid out in *The Little Green Book*:

1. It is not necessary to wipe one's anus with three stones or with three pieces of fabric: a single stone or single piece of fabric is enough.[2]
2. When defecating or urinating, one must squat in such a way as neither to face Mecca nor turn one's back upon it.[3]
3. The meat of horses, mules, or donkeys is not recommended.

It is strictly forbidden if the animal was sodomized by a man (while alive). In that case, the animal must be taken outside the city and sold.[4]

4. If a man becomes aroused by a woman other than his wife but then has intercourse with his own wife, it is preferable for him not to pray if he has sweated; but if he first has intercourse with his spouse and then with another woman, he may say his prayers even though he be in a sweat.[5]

5. If the woman and the man enter the place of worship at the same time and the woman happens to find herself in front of the man, she must say her prayer again after placing herself where she belongs, i.e., behind the man.[6]

6. It is not advisable to allow a feebleminded person, a child, or someone who has just eaten garlic into the mosque.[7]

7. Coughing, belching loudly, or sighing does not invalidate a prayer. On the other hand, the prayer is voided if one emits interjections of two letters or more.[8]

8. If a person who is praying turns red in the face from suppressing an impulse to burst out laughing, that person must start the prayer over again.

9. Clapping one's hands or jumping up in the air during a prayer makes it null and void.[9]

10. If, during prayer, one swallows bits of food left over between one's teeth, the prayer is not invalidated; but if one has a piece of sugar in his mouth and the sugar slowly melts during the prayer, the value of the latter is debatable.[10]

11. One must also avoid praying when one feels sleepy, when one feels an urge to urinate or defecate, or when one is wearing socks that are too tight.[11]

12. If, in order to rescue a person from drowning, one's head becomes immersed during a period of fasting, one's fast is invalidated, even if there was no other way of saving the drowning person's life.[12]

13. If a fly enters the month of a person during a period of

fasting, he is not forced to take it out, if it has not gone too far into the throat; if it has remained in the mouth, he must take it out even if that causes vomiting, which invalidates the fast.[13]

14. If the number of days of the woman's menstrual period is divided by three, a husband who has intercourse with her during the first two days must pay the equivalent of 18 nokhods [about 3 grams or 0.1 ounces] of gold to the poor. . . . Sodomizing a menstruating woman does not require such payment.

15. If a father (or paternal grandfather) marries off his daughter (or granddaughter) in her absence without knowing for a certainty that she is alive, the marriage becomes null and void as soon as it is established that she was dead at the time of the marriage.[14]

16. If a woman who has not reached her ninth birthday or who has not entered menopause gets temporarily married, she must, at the end of the contract or when the husband has released her from part of it, wait two menstrual periods or forty-five days before marrying again.[15]

One of the controversial teachings concerns sexual abuse of minors. The fourth edition of *The Little Green Book* states, "A man can have sexual pleasure from a child as young as a baby. [details deleted] . . . It is better for a girl to marry at such a time when she would begin menstruation at her husband's house, rather than her father's home. Any father marrying his daughter so young will have a permanent place in heaven." I wrestled with whether to include this issue, because of the gross nature of the quote and because a reference to a fourth edition is not widely available.[16]

The translation of this passage has been debated. However, an excerpt from *Hal Ataaka Hadeeth ur-Raafidah* by the late Sheik Abu Musab al-Zargawi who wrote under the alias of "Husayn Al-Musawi" and claimed to have witnessed while Khomeini was living in Iraq, seems to correspond with these teachings.

When it was night time, we were given our supper, and the guests would take the Imam's hand and kiss it, and they would ask him questions. When it was time to sleep, the guests had all left, except for the inhabitants of the house. Khomeini laid his eyes on a young girl who, despite being only four or five years of age, was very beautiful. So the Imam requested from her father, Sayyid Sahib, that he spend the night with her in order to enjoy her. Her father happily agreed, and Imam al-Khomeini spent the night with the girl in his arms, and we could hear her crying and screaming through the night.

These excerpts from *The Little Green Book* are only the tip of the iceberg. Even today, the world is clueless to the author of the 1979 Revolution. One can read article after article about the 1979 Revolution and still know very little about him. This is mainly because so much attention is given to the US embassy hostage crisis that occurred during this time. Some of the writings and quotes by Khomeini are so sick and vile that they cannot be quoted here. Just a few are sufficient to understand what kind of man Khomeini was and what kind of leader the Iranians were subjected to.

However, the supporters of Khomeini who had access to many of these teachings and writings still supported him. The Iranians were not alone, because many Western news outlets seemed just as excited to see what would happen with the rule of Shia Islam. Even though these teachings in *The Little Green Book* were widely circulated, *TIME Magazine* shamelessly named him "Man of the Year" in 1979.

By 1979, Khomeini's religious teachings, like the ones found in his *Little Green Book*, had amassed a large following of passionate young people. The people's discontent with the Shah's government had reached a boiling point. Khomeini offered answers to the grievances of the people and emerged a hero. The Shah no longer had the support of the people, and it was no longer safe for him to remain in Iran. His security could no longer be guaranteed, and out of concern for his safely, he chose to flee from Iran on January 16, 1979.

The Shah's palace in Tehran is now a museum, and when you walk through it you will see that everything in his home was left where it was when he departed. His uniforms and other clothing are still hanging in his closets. There are still family pictures and his wife's belongings. Children's toys still fill the rooms. It seems clear that they planned to return to Iran one day.

About two weeks after the Shah left Iran, Khomeini returned as a victor to cheering crowds, and what happened next changed world history forever.

***

Jimmy Carter was the president of the United States of America. Soon after assuming the presidency, he planned an October surprise. On Halloween in 1977, President Carter, having come to the conclusion that the Central Intelligence Agency (CIA) was too large and powerful, fired the director, George H. W. Bush, along with eight hundred other CIA operatives, an event that became known as the Halloween Massacre. Soon, the US ambassador to Iran, Richard Helms, was replaced. He was also a former director of the CIA and good friends with George H. W. Bush.

The intelligence gathering capabilities of the CIA was thrown out the window along with the eight hundred operatives who were fired. The CIA was scrambling to restructure and train new operatives. President Carter and his cabinet members were feeling around in the dark concerning Iran, which created the perfect environment for Khomeini.

The US Embassy was stormed on February 14—Valentine's Day. Hostages were taken, but after a few hours, Khomeini stepped in, restored order, and released the hostages. The embassy staff was put back in charge.

This should have been a huge wake-up call for the Carter administration, but it was not. The upcoming US elections were the main focus of the government, and the intelligence community was in chaos.

On November 4, 1979, protests erupted outside of the US Embassy, and again hostages were taken, but this time it did not end quickly or peacefully. Again, the president was taken by complete surprise. Suddenly, firing eight hundred CIA agents all at once and being ill-informed about Iran did not seem like such a good idea.

For 444 days, Americans were living a nightmare as images of US hostages were paraded across the TV screen on the evening news. In an attempt to influence US elections, Ayatollah Khomeini agreed to release the hostages only if President Carter lost the election. After 444 days, with the election of Carter's opponent, Ronald Reagan, the hostages were returned to the United States, and the nation began the process of putting the traumatic experience behind them. But the nightmare for the Iranian people was just beginning.

When he came into power, Khomeini instituted a number of changes. Joining the Iranian military or fighting in battle would no longer be just a patriotic duty for Iranians. Under Khomeini, it would be a religious one.

Laws of Iran would not only require civil obedience but would also require religious adherence. Disliking or disagreeing with Khomeini would be equivalent to being rebellious against Allah.

Khomeini would make the national militarization of Islam famous. Khomeini's religious zeal and dedication to the Koran would reach legendary status when he toppled one of the most powerful regimes in the Middle East. He would become a modern-day Islamic version of Melchizedek or a king-priest.

Khomeini was now in charge, and his dream of an Islamic state was becoming a reality.

10
CHRISTIANITY IN IRAN

How many Christians are in Iran?" I asked Daniel (not his real name) as we drove through the city streets in Tehran. Daniel is an Iranian living in Tehran and works with the underground church there.

"I am not sure," he said honestly, which was not the answer that I was looking for. "The church is mainly underground today, and no one really knows." Daniel does not like to talk much. He is more of an administrator who carries out the practical duties of the underground church. He does not like to sit around and debate the different ideas of the church. He would much rather keep his head down and serve the Lord with obedience and humility.

As we drove, he pointed to the old US Embassy that had been taken over in 1979. It remains closed today. The Iranians will open it up from time to time like a museum. "They call the old American Embassy the den of deceit," Daniel said with a slight smile as we drove by. The walls are covered with images of hatred for America. A slightly faded Statue of Liberty can be seen painted on the wall with a skull over Lady Liberty's face.

We turned the corner from the embassy and came to the former location of the Assemblies of God church. It was one of the last Christians churches allowed to operate in Tehran. It was closed.

"The government shut the church down," Daniel said as we passed it. "Too many Iranians were coming to Christ, and their influence became a problem. Muslims are turning their backs on Islam every day, and many of them wanted to come here."

I was astonished. I had seen so many other church buildings throughout the city. Were they all closed? "What about the other churches we saw as we were driving through the city?" I quickly asked.

He paused for a moment. He was still looking at the location where Assemblies of God used to be. Daniel went there as a young believer after he was released from the Iranian army. "Oh, those are not Iranian churches. They are mostly Armenian, but even the Armenian churches are heavily restricted. Today most of them are only allowed to be open for cultural weddings and ceremonies."

It is impossible to tell the story of Christianity in Iran without talking about the Armenians. The Armenians continue to be one of the most present representatives of Christianity in Iran today. Iranians know that Armenians are Christian by culture, but few of them know why. Even most Armenians don't know why.

In the spring of 2012, Pastor Billy Humphrey from International House of Prayer, Atlanta, came with me and several Chinese pastors from the underground house church in China to attend a meeting in the country of Georgia, in its capital city, Tbilisi. After the meeting, we decided to take a trip across the border to Armenia to meet with some people to talk about ministry to the Iranians.

Immediately, Pastor Billy and I could tell that Armenia was nothing like its neighbor, Georgia. Georgia broke away from the Russians in 1991 and created an independent state with close ties to the United States and Europe. The economy of Georgia had visible signs of growth. Armenia also gained independence in 1991 but remained tied to the Soviet Union. It still has the appearance of an old Soviet block and is swimming in poverty. From the moment that we crossed the border in our small car, we could see the difference.

Not long after arriving in Armenia, we were able to make our way to Khor Virap. Khor Virap is a monastery that sits at the base of Mount Ararat where Noah's ark is said to have come to rest

(Genesis 8:4). Khor Virap is not just any monastery. It is a location that changed history for the Armenian people.

The monastery was absolutely beautiful with snow-capped Mount Ararat as the backdrop. Mount Ararat sits on the border of Turkey, Armenia, and Iran. In the third century, a missionary of Iranian (Parthian) descent who later became known as Gregory the Illuminator traveled to Armenia to share the Good News of Jesus Christ.

He refused to worship the pagan gods of the Armenian king. As a result, he was tortured, given the death penalty, and thrown into a pit at the base of Mount Ararat, which many people believe is close to where Noah first offered a sacrifice to God.

Gregory sat in the pit for more than thirteen years and was completely forgotten by almost everyone. He was not supposed to survive, but God provided food from a pious woman who lowered it down to him every day.

Unbeknownst to Gregory, the king contracted an incurable disease, went insane, and was about to die. His sister had a dream about Gregory and was told in the dream that only Gregory's God could heal her brother. Everyone thought she was crazy because everyone was certain that Gregory was dead.

The royal guard traveled to the pit at her orders and was astonished to find Gregory alive. They pulled him out and begged him to pray for the king. He did, and the king was healed of the disease. After being healed, the king declared, "Your God is my God."

A decree was issued that all Armenians would worship Jesus Christ.

The history of the miracle at Khor Virap and Gregory's faithfulness continues to have an impact on Iran today. God continues to use the Armenians to shine the light of Christ amidst the darkness of Iran.

Armenians know the true meaning of persecution. Long before their persecution in Iran, they were being exterminated by the hundreds of thousands in Turkey. The term *genocide* was actually coined to describe the atrocities against the Armenian Christians when the Turks declared holy jihad against them. Children were kidnapped and given to Muslim families and forced to convert. Women were raped and sent to live as slaves in harems. As many as three out of every four Armenians were killed.

Today, however, many of the ministries that have had some of the most impact on Iranians on the ground have been led to Christ by Armenians.

Very few organizations in the world today have the level of impact and influence in Iran as Elam Ministries. Elam Ministries was started in the United Kingdom in 1990 and is run by Sam Yeghnazar. Sam was born in Iran but is of Armenian descent.

I met Sam for the first time in Turkey in 2011 right after a major earthquake hit the city of Van. He was hosting a seminar to assist Iranians who were able to travel to Turkey to get the training they needed as well as the essential tools necessary to support the underground house churches. All of the students at the training were from Iran and were training for Iranian ministry. Back to Jerusalem provided many of the goods that were needed on the ground in Van to help the earthquake victims.

Sam's father, Seth, was born and raised in a Christian Armenian family in Iran. His father rededicated his life to Christ in his early twenties and became a worker for the Bible Society. He was able to get his hands on magazines produced by Oral Roberts, whose writings had a great influence on him in his early years. Sam's father started an underground house church where many Armenians and Assyrians attended, but Seth reached out specifically to Iranians. There was a fresh focus on the power of the Holy Spirit at these house church meetings. Sam and his siblings grew up seeing this example of a father in his home.

Two of Sam's brothers also run ministries focused on Iranians. Many well-known Iranians who were eventually martyred for their faith came to Christ in Seth's home.

I have had the privilege to work indirectly with both Sam and his brother Lazarus for several years through the Chinese ministry of Back to Jerusalem.

Lazarus is actively involved with training leaders and continues to remain optimistic about the Christian future of Iran. We met when I was in London putting together a team to repair one of their training facilities. "The church is growing so fast," he said. "It is not a matter of if the regime will fall but when the regime will fall, and the Christians have to ask themselves if they are ready to operate in a post Islamic government in Iran."

Armenian Christians, like those of the Yeghnazar family, continue to operate and suffer the persecution that is taking place among the Christians in Iran. However, the Armenian Christians are not an exact reflection of what is happening among the ethnic Muslim Iranians.

To see what is happening among the Iranian population in Iran, we will have to dig a little deeper, because what I have found is one of the most amazing stories in world history that has yet to be told.

11
CHRISTIAN REVIVAL IN IRAN

The Islamic Revolution in Iran changed the situation for Christians. There were very few Christians prior to the Revolution, but after the Revolution, policies were put in place to remove Christianity completely from Iran. Those efforts were implemented by the highest authorities in Iran and systematically enforced. But after more than thirty years of Sharia Law, the Muslim leadership has failed to abolish Christianity from Iran.

Instead, Iran has given birth to the most vibrant and dynamic church that has ever existed in the history of the country. In fact, the new believers in Iran are some of the most well-versed opponents of Islam and can intelligently dissect it to reveal the evils of the Koran and the truth of the Bible.

Iran banned Bibles that have been translated in native languages but has cautiously allowed it in other languages, thinking Iranians would not want to learn what are often thought of as inferior languages. However, the Bible is now one of the most sought-after books in Iran.

The revival in Iran is messy, but it is vibrant. It looks muddled and disheveled, but it is contagious and exciting. To truly understand the revival that is taking place, it would be good to visit the Grand Bazaar in Tehran, because in many ways, the Iranian revival feels like a bazaar. To the Western mind, the revival in Iran does not make sense. The Grand Bazaar can have the same initial effect because it is confusing, endlessly zigzagging, and seemingly without order.

When my taxi dropped me off at the Grand Bazaar in Tehran in 2014, I attempted to explore it on my own. I allotted myself about thirty minutes to walk through it. I thought thirty minutes would be plenty of time.

I could not have been more wrong! I had been to bazaars in Istanbul and even in China's Xinjiang province, but nothing could have prepared me for the bazaar in Tehran. I quickly became disoriented in a labyrinth that lacked any reference points.

The corridors of the Grand Bazaar are over ten kilometers. It is a city within a city; a culture within a culture. The bazaar has everything one could ever need or hope for. Every turn, every corridor, and every shop are like new microcosms of experience with their own enclave, inviting you in for warm tea and exotic shopping.

The aromas danced through the air and waited for me at every turn. The sheer size of the bazaar was difficult for me to wrap my mind around.

The revival in Iran is very much like the initial confusion and daunting mystery of the Grand Bazaar in Iran. Initially, there is a strong desire to find reference points or identify familiar sights and to create order out of the chaos. But the revival in Iran has not followed the same pattern of modern revivals.

Iran's revival is not taking place in tents or modern church buildings. Camera crews are not standing by ready to document every service. The leadership inside is not writing books or teaching seminars about how to have a revival. Instead, the revival is taking place in homes, some of which are in a series of house church networks throughout Iran.

The church meetings are not advertised on billboards, and they do not have an event page posted on the Internet. Instead, the believers are meeting in secret. The revival is taking place among family members and friends. The glory of God is falling upon the Iranians in their kitchens where they eat their meals and in their rooms where they sleep at night.

Some of the believers who meet together do not even share their real names. Bible names are often adopted as separate identities to keep other believers safe from being tortured for information. Although the believers are cautious, meeting secretly in underground house churches does not mean they are denying the name of Jesus or not sharing their faith with others. Far from it.

The revival in Iran is fueled by the zealous and aggressive evangelism of the Iranian believers who have traded the darkness of Islam for the truth of Jesus Christ. Traditionally in Iran, church leadership was held by Assyrian or Armenian Christians, but today there is a sense of Iranian ownership in the evangelism and outreach among the growing house churches.

Prior to the Islamic Revolution, Iran had very few Iranian Christians, but now, under extreme Islamic rule, more Iranians are coming to Christ than any other Muslim country in the world.

It is clear to us at Back to Jerusalem that the demand for Bibles in Iran is growing because the number of Iranians becoming Christians is growing. There is a huge revival taking place in Iran today, and it is changing the landscape of the country.

Many people ask, "How many believers are now in Iran?" There are many numbers that are floating around, so it is best to stay conservative.

Conservatively, there were roughly only two to three hundred Iranian MBBs (Muslim Background Believers, Christians from Muslim families) in 1977.[1]

After the Islamic Revolution, not much is known about those believers, but the best one can estimate would be the following:

Growth of Iranian Christians after 1977:

1978	1990	1994	1999	2003
200–300	8,000	18,000	27,500	30,000[2]

Those numbers do not reflect the Armenian church or the Assyrian church, whose numbers can be as many as 250,000 members.

Today, the underground house church numbers fluctuate dramatically.

A close look into the situation will reveal why there is little idea of the number of Christians in Iran.

The primary problem is that there aren't enough people on the ground representing foreign ministries. The cold, hard truth that few Christian ministries want to admit is that there is a lack of people on the ground. The number of ministries promoting their work in Iran is numerous, but those with actual people on the ground who are free to travel in and out of the country and speak to supporters are few. Because of this deficiency, it is difficult to determine the actual number of Christians in Iran as well as the amount of resources available and the progress that is being made to spread the Gospel.

More Christian missionaries are needed in Iran. The impact of Christian satellite TV, radio, and the Internet in Iran has been phenomenal, but the impact is limited because of the lack of face-to-face interaction between believers on the ground.

I was a trained infantryman in the military, and I feel that there is an incalculable value of putting people on the ground. Push-button warfare is unable to replace boots on the ground. Even the American military, with access to the most powerful bombs in the world, the most sophisticated drones, and crystal-clear photos from satellite images, cannot advance without men on the ground.

Christian mission organizations engaged in spiritual warfare can learn a lot from military strategists. Here is one quote that mission organizations today would benefit a great deal from: "You may fly over a land forever; you may bomb it, atomize it, pulverize it and wipe it clean of life—but if you desire to defend it, protect it and keep it for civilization, you must do this on the ground, the way the Roman legions did, by putting your young men in the mud" (T. R. Fehrenbach).

Another challenge when calculating the number of believers in Iran is the fact that church activity is illegal in Iran, which means that Christians are not registering their gathering places or keeping track of their numbers. The less information gathered, the safer things are for everyone.

The third reason why the number of Christians is not clear is because many Christians in Iran today do not know they are Christians! Many believers in Iran do not know they are considered followers of Christ because they do not own a Bible or know any Christians but have come to Christ in a dream! (We will discuss this further in the next chapter.) This is a crazy phenomenon that makes it extremely difficult when calculating the number of believers in Iran today.

Despite all these challenges, organizations and ministries are doing their best to estimate the growing number of believers in Iran.

World Christian Database counted 66,000 Protestants in Iran in 2010. In the same year, Open Doors estimated 370,000 Muslim background believers. The United Nations Refugee Agency that deals with Christian asylum seekers on a regular basis estimates a total of 250,000 Christians in Iran.

In 2013, Back to Jerusalem was told by an underground house church leader involved in distribution of materials to the numerous house churches that there were at least half a million believers in and around the capital city of Tehran.

"Half of the population would desert Islam if they had the freedom to do so," said Abe Ghaffari, the director of Iranian Christians International.

Lazarus Yeghnazar, the leader of 222 ministries, now based in Great Britain, stated, "In the last 20 years, more Iranians have come to Christ compared to the last fourteen centuries."

The 2013 Operation World prayer manual listed the growth of Christianity in Iran as leading the entire world, with approximately 20 percent annual growth. This means that the Christian church in Iran is doubling every four or five years. At present growth rates, this would mean that in ten short years, roughly one in ten Iranians will be a follower of Jesus. In twenty years, half of the nation could be Christian. Consider the changes to the region if this revival continues.

If 300,000 is a number that can be agreed upon (more conservative than the Open Doors estimate), then that would mean that there is a Muslim background believer coming to Christ in Iran every hour. However, Back to Jerusalem, based on in-country resources, estimates that the number of Muslim background believers is much higher than 300,000, which means that the number of Muslims coming to Christ could be as high as fifty per day.

In proportion to the population in Iran, the number of people coming to Christ in a Muslim country is amazing. In practice, this roughly means that for every Christian who dies or is put in prison in Iran, at least one thousand people come to Christ.

The young men and women running to Christ in Iran are looking for something that fills the emptiness in their souls. They are not looking to overthrow the Iranian government. They are not looking to start a political revolution. Among all the Christians I have met in Iran, not one time have I heard them discuss the overthrow of the current leadership.

These new Christians are not a part of a political movement with grand ideas to mimic the Occupy Wall Street movement. They merely want to worship the God of light and truth and turn from the demons of darkness and despair.

One of the main characteristics of the revival in Iran today that some Christians might be uncomfortable with is that it is very charismatic in nature. Singing, praying out loud, and even dancing can be seen and heard in the Iranian churches. There is a strong reliance on the work of the Holy Spirit.

Unlike the Greek heritage of the church in Rome that relied heavily on logic and cognitive reasoning, the church in Iran is seeing more of a mystical phenomenon that is connected to the history of the land.

Is persecution driving the revival, or is it something deeper?

From my observation, the revival's germination is something that will blow the mind of most readers. It is something that could not have been planned for or included in a mission budget. I believe the revival in Iran is being fueled by a mystical phenomenon—dreams.

The power that dreams are having on church growth in Iran is changing history.

12
DREAMS

I would like to state that I am not much into visions and dreams. In Christian circles, I am in the minority. After serving for more than fifteen years in the underground house church in China, I am an endangered species. I personally dislike the idea of living life based on a vision or a dream. I am not saying that it is wrong; I am only saying that I don't like it because it doesn't make sense to me.

I like things that I can touch, taste, smell, or measure. I like things that I can observe or hold in my hands. I watch TV shows where people are explaining to others what their dreams mean or I listen to Christians talk about the iconology of dreams, and I try to learn, but I can't help but feel like an outsider because those ideas are so far from my own reality.

If I have an intense dream about driving a car through a crowd of Africans riding on pandas speaking Persian, the first thing that I assume when I wake up is that I ate too much chili the night before. I do not assume that God is trying to speak to me or that something in my dream is pointing to an omen in my future.

Prophetic interpretations can really make me nervous. One time I traveled to see a mission director in the southern part of the United States who has since become a good friend of mine. We were supposed to spend some time together speaking about mission work. Instead, he had set up for me an appointment with a room full of prophets. I was sure that it was a gag. Anyone who knows me knows that I believe that God uses prophets greatly, but I like to observe; I do not participate.

"Eugene, we are just going to go up to our prayer room and spend time with you and see what God is saying over your life," my friend said to me as we stepped into the elevator. Eight other people joined us in the elevator. They all looked at me and smiled, knowing I was going to be their pet project for the day. They were the team of prophets, otherwise known as the "God Squad," who were tasked with praying over me.

I was nervous and felt out of place. "So . . . where are you guys from?" I asked as we waited for the elevator to move. I have lived in Hong Kong for almost half of my life, where time is short, people are busy, and the elevators move like roller coasters. After experiencing Hong Kong elevators, American elevators feel like they take a lifetime to move up or down. Someone needed to break the silence on the slow American elevator.

"Shhh," one of the women kindly responded. "We prefer it better if we do not know anything about you." I was suddenly reminded of the mad professor from the movie *Back to the Future*. The professor has an electronic gadget on his head, and whenever Marty tries to talk and explain why he is there, the professor yells, "No! Don't tell me!" He wanted to read Marty's mind with his gadget. That was how I was feeling.

When we arrived at the prayer room, I was encircled by Christians with prophetic gifts. They began to pray. Some of them sang. Others remained silent with their eyes closed. A few of them made strange sounds as they cried out to God in prayer. I brought my hands up to my mouth as if to show that I was praying, but I kept my eyes open. As a teenager, I learned at Bible camp in Indiana that praying with your eyes open ensured that no one would steal food from your plate while others were saying grace.

Then something even more strange began to happen. Some of them began to have visions, and then they used those visions to draw pictures in what they called prophetic art. I had never seen anyone have a vision and then draw what they saw in their vision. Those with visions spoke and prayed in the most powerful way imaginable. They made a special deposit into my life.

It was then, in that room, that I understood what I did not understand, what I still do not understand fully. God has given special gifts to everyone, and He speaks to us in unique ways according to the way that He made us and in line with the gifts He has put in our lives.

Several years later in April 2013, I found myself on a book tour in a church in Norway. I started the evening talking about the underground church in North Korea, the subject of the book that I was promoting.

However, knowing that a group of Iranians were in the back of the room listening, I began to talk about the similarities between underground churches in China, North Korea, and Iran. I briefly mentioned the people in Iran coming to Christ because of visions and dreams. All of the Iranians began to laugh among themselves in the back of the room. Suddenly I felt very self-conscious and wondered if they thought that the idea was laughable. I had just come from Iran and knew about many people coming to Christ because of dreams. Perhaps this group of young Iranians found the idea preposterous.

At the end of the service, I approached them and eventually built up the courage to ask them why they laughed when I talked about Iranians coming to Christ through dreams. The interpreter for the Iranian group immediately shared with me that all of the Iranians in the group were led to Christ by one person and that person came to Christ because of a dream!

The phenomenon is happening seemingly every day in Iran. It doesn't matter how *I* feel about dreams or visions, because dreams and visions are changing Iran.

There is a devaluation of dreams in the Western world and a dismissive attitude regarding their significance, but throughout the Bible, dreams revealed divine meanings and acted as a method of communication between God and His people. Dreams were fraught with meaning about the future, offered solutions to life's biggest problems, or warned of imminent dangers.

Today, many people believe that dreams are a physical manifestation of a psychological state—that dreams are connected to experiences, exposure, traumatic events, or even indigestion. However, the ancients considered dreams to be sacred and religious. And in Iran, dreams and visions are having just as much power as they did ages ago. Thousands of lives are being changed, and the landscape of an entire country is being transformed because of the power of dreams.

In June 2014, I was in the United Kingdom and had the rare opportunity to sit down with a well-known British pastor who is ordained with the Church of England. He has had a lot of experience with international outreach with both charismatic and conservative church movements. Today he is the director of a ministry focused on sharing the Gospel message with Muslims.

"You know," I said, excited to have an opportunity to be talking with him, "I have been working a lot lately with Iranian Christians and . . ." I paused for a moment. I didn't know how to quite say that many of them have been coming to Christ through dreams. Although he is no longer an officer in the Royal Artillery as he once was, he still has a very commanding presence about him. I felt a bit foolish suggesting that dreams were a dominant reason for Iranians coming to Christ. I almost wanted to whisper it across the table.

But I really wanted to hear his opinion on the phenomenon. He works with Muslims on a regular basis and travels in completely different circles from me. I was really eager to know if I was working in a microcosm, or if he too had been exposed to Muslim believers who had come to Christ through a dream.

"Well . . . many of them—many of them claim—that they are coming to Christ through dreams." I watched his face for a response to my statement.

I was very surprised at his reaction. "Oh, yes. It is true."

"Wow. So you have been seeing this too?" I responded, feeling more confident now.

"I would say 100 percent of all of the Iranians that we are working with in Oxford have come to Christ either directly or indirectly because of a dream."

I was astonished. One hundred percent is an extraordinary claim, but again and again, it was being confirmed that Iranians were being impacted through their dreams.

This was all new to me, but the truth is, the ancient world of Iran and the biblical culture of the Jews embraced dreams. They found meaning and direction from the mysterious open doors of dreams that occur during the vulnerability of the night. These dreams open up fantastic windows of fleeting reality that are very different from the world that they attempt to manage during the day.

During the day, we toil and labor to maintain control and exert our authority and dominion over the world around us. Insurance companies make billions of dollars providing for our insatiable desire for control and protection from unforeseen future disasters in attempts to be less vulnerable.

Unfortunately for those who seek control, sleep awaits us all. No insurance plan or amount of planning can keep any one of us from the same vulnerability that was encountered by the ancient world.

The world we manage when we are awake will not submit when we slumber. We have experiences that we do not initiate and events that we cannot control. In our dreams, we are not as restricted as we are during the day. Even if we are aged or handicapped, in our dreams, we can run, fall, fight, and climb. We fall in love, lust, and sometimes we unleash such unbridled rage on even our most loved ones that we feel the guilt when we awake. Helplessness, loss, and even death visit more frequently than they do in the work fields of daylight.

The ancients put more value on the meaning of dreams than we do today. Dreams invaded the sleep of the mighty and powerful Pharaoh. His guards could not protect him or keep the dreams at bay. Joseph, the imprisoned slave, was allowed to interpret the dreams.

Likewise, the laws of Islam that are keeping Christian missionaries and biblical literature out of Iran are defenseless against dreams. Because of the Koran, the Iranian people are aware of Jesus. The Koran mentions the name of Jesus, or Isa, as He is called, several times. In fact, the Koran mentions the name of Jesus more times than it does the name of Muhammad. Also, several Koranic Surahs refer to Jesus as Jesus Christ.

Christ was not Jesus' last name. It was His title!

The Koran also mentions the virgin birth and that Jesus, the son of Mary, was sent by God.

So when Iranian Muslims have dreams about Jesus, many of them are able to recognize Him as the Isa of the Koran.

I have talked to many Iranians who have come to Christ because of a dream. None of them have ever told me that Jesus came to them in their dream, asked them to repeat the "sinner's prayer," and then label themselves as a "Christian."

To most Iranians, the term *Christian* is very culturally significant as well as religiously. When an Iranian tells another Iranian that they have become a Christian, they are often understood as having become an Armenian. To the normal Iranian, being Christian and being an Armenian are the same thing. How can an Iranian ever become an Armenian?

Many Iranians who experience Christ in a dream have to mentally process several things. They do not just go to sleep one evening and wake up the next morning as a Christian, ready to attend Sunday morning service with their families. They have years of propaganda to combat. They have been told their entire lives that Christians are evil like the Jews. They have been told that Christians follow three gods and that Jesus was a prophet like Muhammad. They have been told that the apostle Paul was a liar and corrupted the Bible and that only the Koran is pure.

Most of the Iranians who tell me about their dreams tell me that their lives changed because of the process after the dream. Instead of experiencing complete conversion in the dream, the dreams have acted as a catalyst in the process of searching and discovery. Iranians are meeting with Jesus or seeing Jesus in their dreams, and their lives are changed forever. They do not wake up knowing more but instead wake up *wanting* to know more.

The dreams ignited a sudden desire to find a Bible or to find a Christian to help explain their dreams to them. They start seeking answers to the many questions in their dreams.

The dreams are not an end result but a starting point to follow Jesus. Because of the cultural connotations associated with the term *Christian*, many Iranians who come to Christ because of a dream think of themselves as followers of Jesus but do not label themselves *Christian*. This is an important difference.

These new Iranian believers who might not refer to themselves as Christians but are following Christ are willing, and sometimes required, to give their lives for Christ. As believers in the Gospel, they are subjected to unemployment, persecution, divorce, loss of contact with family, and imprisonment. Apostasy, or turning away from Islam, is grounds for the death penalty.

Missionary work is banned in Iran, and many churches and mission organizations are afraid of the consequences of working in an environment that is so dangerous. Jesus said very clearly in Matthew 28:19, "Go therefore and make disciples of all nations." No exemption was given for those countries that would not allow the Good News of Jesus Christ. Dreams are working where the church has clearly failed in Iran.

13

IRAN'S CHRISTIAN PERSECUTION

I was a teacher in Iran," Sarah (not her real name) said. "I have seen the persecution and how Iran uses teachers to get to the children." Sarah is an Iranian refugee living in Sweden, which has been a refuge for many Iranians like Sarah.

We were having a simple summer meal in Stockholm. Like many other western European countries, Sweden has received plane loads of Iranian refugees. According to the most recent available data, there are more than fifty-five thousand first-generation Iranians living in Sweden.[1] The second generation of Iranians are already well established and make up one of Sweden's largest immigrant populations, with Iranians being nearly one out of every one hundred Swedes.

"As a teacher in Iran," Sarah continued, "I was told to play games with the children and spy into their family through communicating with them. I would ask questions like, 'So, what do you do at your home for fun? Do your parents ever have secret parties where friends and family members come over?'" Sarah paused as she searched for the English words. "My job was to find out if they were having Bible studies or Christian meetings in their home. I was taught to use the children to go home and get more information for me and bring it back to the school. The children didn't know that I was actually using them. They trusted me. I was their teacher. In Iran, the teachers are trusted by the students, and the teachers are trained to use that trust to use the children for information. It's so sad, because the students would do anything to make the teacher happy."

As we continued to eat our lunch, there were other Iranians at the table who had similar stories as Sarah. Sarah is not the first refugee to find a support network in Sweden. Unlike other minorities in Sweden who have obtained refugee status, Iranians like Sarah are trained professionals. In fact, in Sweden, as well as in other parts of Europe, Iranians are overrepresented in higher education and in high-paying professions like dentistry and engineering.

Sarah, along with every other Iranian at the table that afternoon, did not have a desire to live in Sweden. Instead, she was forced to leave her home country and finally ended up in Sweden because living in Iran was too dangerous.

As Sarah knows all too well, there is a war in the spiritual realm in Iran, and not even children are off limits. This war is not new. It started on the day that Islam marched onto Iranian soil and was solidified through the Islamic Revolution of 1979.

***

Soon after the Revolution, any commitment that the Ayatollah made with the church immediately vanished. The Islamic government went on the offensive right away and began persecuting Christians. Churches were closed, clergy were arrested, pastors were thrown into prisons, missionaries were kicked out, and even hospitals were raided and labeled as bases for spy activity.

Because relief work was associated with Christians, applications for humanitarian visas were rejected. Anti-Christian and anti-Jewish rhetoric was ramped up to levels not seen since Nazi Germany.

When Iraq attacked Iran, the Islamic leadership found themselves in a situation where it better served their purposes to appease the Christians living in Iran, but the tone had definitely been set.

The Iranian constitution guarantees that religious rights are protected, but it is important to understand that these rights are viewed through the eyes of Islam.

What Islam recognizes as religious rights or freedom of religion and what a Christian recognizes as freedom of religion are two completely different things.

For the Muslim, freedom is defined as something that is only available to the followers of Allah, but not necessarily to the individual. Christians see freedom as accessible to the individual.

The philosophy of an individual's value in Islam is based on the community, and Iranians earn merit from adherence to the Koran. In other words, the Iranians see an individual's worth in a group setting.

The oppressed have no rights in Islam unless the oppressed are Muslim. Any recognition that is given to a non-Muslim is considered to be charitable, not a right. The non-believer has no right to lay claim to anything.

Many Christians today who consider themselves to be more tolerant will argue that Islam should not be judged by the actions of a few. However, it must be established from the beginning that the problems in Iran are attributed to the spirit of Islam—not the minority understanding of Islam, but the understanding of the majority as is practiced in every Muslim country. The spirit of Islam is the enemy of Jesus Christ. There is just no pretty way to say it. Universal justice and righteousness for the rights of non-Muslims are not inherent in Islam. But it is also important to point out that Muslims are not the enemy of Christians; Islam is. Muslims are the target of Jesus' love.

The *oppressed*, as referred to in the Koran, refers to the oppressed followers of Islam. If Muslims do not fight for their rights under Islam, then they are thought of as sinners. If the oppressed do not resist and fight the oppressor, then they will be punished in the afterlife (Surah 4:97). Christian teaching, even as a minority religion, is considered to be offensive and must be opposed by Muslims. Persecution starts here.

There is a teaching of entitlement among the Muslims, and any Muslim who is kept from that entitlement must meet the oppressor with aggression. Muslims, according to the Koran, are entitled to superior status, and when they are not recognized as superior, it is their duty to fight for it. This is one of the main reasons why Danish cartoons and Israeli occupation can result quickly in violent eruptions, protests, attacks on embassies and civilians, as well as suicide bombings.

The lack of recognition of individual rights can be further seen in an Islamic economy. Individual ownership is not a Muslim concept. Property and wealth are considered to be community property in Iran.

Clergy members are at the top, and those who are on the bottom (in a Muslim society) should be happy with their lot and not strive to have more (Surah 59:7).

It is believed that everything belongs to Allah anyway and, by proxy, his representatives on earth.

When Muslims cry out for freedom, it is not the same as a Christian may perceive it. The language is the same, but the concepts are completely different.

In a nutshell, a Muslim's idea of freedom is freedom from oppression, but still within the Islamic setting. In Iran, Islam cannot be considered the source of any oppression. Freedom from Islam is impossible and unthinkable.

In Iran, the voice of the individual is almost nonexistent. This is not because the government of Iran is Iranian; it is because the government of Iran is Islamic. This is not a theory or a Christian-biased indictment on Islam but rather a logical conclusion from observing Islamic countries, including Iran, both past and present. Iran is ruled by Islamic law, and Islamic law is the antithesis of freedom. The less Islamic law that is adopted for a society, the more likely freedom might be an option for the people. The reverse is also true, whether it be Saudi Arabia, Egypt, Pakistan, Indonesia, Malaysia, or Turkey.

Islam is the root cause of persecution of Christians in Iran today. In Iranian Islamic law, that is both expounded on and enforced by the Ayatollah, it is spelled out that non-Muslims have a clear second-class status. Once Sharia Law was incorporated into the Iranian legal system, religious and gender-based persecution became part of the legal structure. Christians have no rights in the legal sense. The constitution of Iran in articles 13 and 14 only provides the charitable notion that religious minorities are protected, but any serious attempt to litigate on the basis of religious rights is futile because no real rights are actually spelled out in articles 13 and 14.

According to Article 14 of the Iranian constitution, "In accordance with the sacred verse, Allah does not forbid you to deal kindly and justly with those who have not fought against you because of your religion and who have not expelled you from their homes" (60:8).

So according to Article 14, Allah does not forbid treating others kindly and justly? How nice of him not to *forbid* it. But apparently he does not actively endorse it either. Compare this to the words of Jesus: "But I say to you, Love your enemies, and pray for those who persecute you" (Matthew 5:44). Jesus commands His followers to love their enemies.

Article 23 of the Iranian constitution states, "The investigation of the individuals' beliefs is forbidden, and no one may be molested or taken to task simply for holding a certain belief." That notion, however, is quickly squashed in Article 167, which gives judges ultimate discretion to implement the rulings of the grand Ayatollah, which is death for anyone who coverts from Islam.

The Iranian Muslims do not see Christians as being oppressed because in their teaching, only Muslims can be oppressed. The Jews and the Christians can never be equal, and in the Islamic context, this is not injustice.

The non-believer needs to practice the art of submission.

Failure to submit or convert is considered an act of aggression against Islam, and aggression is met with aggression, leading to the persecution that is seen almost every day in Iran. Peaceful Islam sounds pretty and unifying in public speeches and on political campaign trails, but it does not actually exist when confronted with one who refuses to submit or convert to Islam.

It is not a mystery why there is Christian persecution in Iran today. The manifestation of oppression can be seen in everyday life. For instance, non-Muslim grocery-store owners are required to indicate their religious affiliation on the front of their shops, and to attend higher-education institutions, one must pass a Sharia Law exam. Christians in the workplace and factories are told that they cannot touch certain things that will be used by Muslims. The Ayatollah Khomeini believed that Christians, unlike Muslims, have the capacity to contaminate, and today many Iranians refuse to eat at restaurants where Christians might serve.

In June 1993, the Iranian government ordered all Christian churches to sign a statement that would forbid them to evangelize to Muslims. The government went even further and laid out rules that made biblical worship illegal in Iran. When I first read the charter, I was amazed at the similarities between the charter and the rules implemented through the Three-Self, or government-controlled church of China. In China, the persecution comes from the atheistic beliefs enforced by the Communist Party. In Iran, the persecution comes from the Islamic beliefs enforced by the Iranian government. In both cases, the characteristics were very similar.

The Iranian Christian Church leadership was ordered to sign an agreement that stated:

1. Church services could not be held in Persian, the official language of Iran.
2. Church members must be issued membership cards and produce them upon attendance.
3. Membership lists, complete with addresses, must be

handed over to government authorities.

4. Meetings must be confined to Sunday, not Friday, the officially recognized day of Muslim worship.
5. Only members could attend Sunday meetings.
6. New members could only be added to the membership and admitted to the meetings once the Ministry of Culture and Islamic Guidance had been notified.

Shockingly, every church leader in Iran signed it except for two. One of the leaders who refused to sign the agreement was Pastor Haik Hovsepian. Pastor Haik was harassed and persecuted for not telling the United Nations that there was religious freedom in Iran. A few months later, Pastor Haik vanished from Tehran and was later found stabbed to death.

Many observers point out that Iran votes for their leadership, which leads many to believe that Iran is a democratic country. The assumption is made that the people could change their systematic persecution of Christians if they wanted to. Can't an electorate be persuaded to abandon persecution and merely vote for leadership that stands on the side of Christians? The answer to that question depends on how you define democracy.

In a democratic system, whether it is direct or representative, the government is voted in by the people. The ultimate power is vested in the people and exercised directly by the people or their elected representatives.

"Is Iran a democratic country?" I asked one of the well-known tour guides in Tehran who is well versed in Iranian history and its politics. The tour guide paused for a moment and then pulled out his folder with laminated charts and showed me what all of the tour guides in Iran are given to explain the democratic process. Here is a simple picture from my camera phone of what is given by the government to explain the Iranian government to tourists.

I was confused by the chart. There are arrows going all around that make it seem as though all things are decided by the people when, in fact, all things are decided by the Supreme Leader.

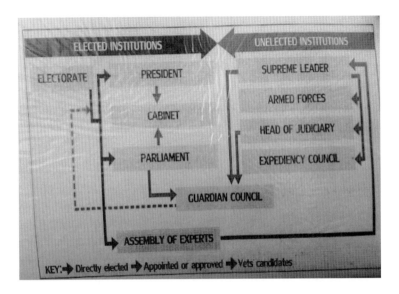

When Iran was having presidential elections in 2013, all the major news networks were debating what changes would take place if "reformer" Hassan Rouhani were to win the presidency. There was excitement everywhere about how the new president might open up new roads of diplomacy that the former president had closed. Christians working in Iran and praying for Iran even began to discuss the changes that could occur, especially with regard to persecution, if a reformer like Hassan Rouhani was elected.

But in truth, nothing was going to change because of the presidential election, because the president holds very little power in Iran and is preselected by the Supreme Leader. The elections mean very little.

The presidential candidates are selected by the Guardian Council, and the members of the Guardian Council are selected by the Supreme Leader. Technically, the Supreme Leader selects only six of the twelve members that serve on the Guardian Council, but the other six are selected by Parliament members who are selected by the Head of Judicial Power, who is also selected by the Supreme Leader.

You see the conundrum? It is a power structure all leading back to the Supreme Leader. The president actually only has the power given to him by the Supreme Leader. The people are only able to vote for candidates who are preselected, either directly or indirectly, by the Supreme Leader.

According to the chart, the Assembly of Experts, or Islamic theologians, appears to have the power to select the Supreme Leader, but in reality, it does not. The Supreme Leader also selects the Assembly of Experts, and the one time in history that a new Supreme Leader was chosen by the Assembly of Experts, fulfilling their only real duty, the current Supreme Leader rejected the selection and another "more suitable" Supreme Leader was chosen. Ayatollah Montazeri was appointed as the successor to Khomeini, but Khomeini dismissed him, and soon Ayatollah Ali Hosseini Khamenei was chosen.

The Ayatollah is not the president, but he holds all of the power. Westerners often confuse the title of president and assume that the president of Iran must be the one in charge when the president has been vetted by the Supreme Leader before he was even a candidate.

The persecution in Iran is directed from the top down, and the people are politically powerless to change it without the miraculous intervention of Jehovah.

If the Iranian media, an important part of the political machinery, wanted to report and tell the people what is happening during their elections, they would not be able to because it is all controlled by the state. The media that is not state owned has to get their content approved by the state.

Again, this is another measure of control by the Supreme Leader that enables the continual persecution of Christians. Even Iran's telecommunication companies are almost entirely state owned, and records are available to the Supreme Leader to track down Christian leaders or Muslim converts Telecommunications is one of the main weapons used in the persecution war against Christians in Iran, and there is one who knows that well: Kashi (not his real name).

I met Kashi when he was pastoring the only Iranian church allowed to operate in Van, in eastern Turkey. In 2011, Turkey experienced a massive earthquake, and we were working together to help the people of Van. Kashi was an Iranian refugee who escaped to Turkey with his family. He had only been in Turkey for less than a year when I met him.

On December 26, 2010, before he fled to Turkey, he and his family boarded a train to attend Christian meetings in Tehran. The following morning when he arrived in the capital city of Tehran, he received a phone call. The call was coming from his own home. He was traveling with his wife and his nine-year-old daughter, so everyone who lived in his home was with him. The call didn't make any sense.

"Hello?" he said when he answered the phone.

"May I speak to Mr. Kashi? This is the police."

"This is Mr. Kashi, how can I help you?"

"I am sorry to report to you that your home has been broken into and you need to return home immediately to make a report."

Something about the information being given by the officer didn't seem right. The officer could not really give details about how he knew about the crime, who had reported it, what had been taken, etc. Immediately, Kashi hung up and called his neighbor, who was a fellow believer. The neighbor told him the police had raided Kashi's home and were taking computers, books, and other items out of his house. They had set up a trap for him and wanted him to come back so they could arrest him.

Kashi knew the police must have found out that he was a pastor. Thus began life on the run for Kashi and his family.

He immediately contacted one of his underground church friends in Tehran, and he and his family went into hiding there. After only a short time, the police raided the place where he was staying, but Kashi and his family got away. Kashi was able to find a new location and go into hiding there, but soon the police raided that location as well. Kashi and his family were again able to escape.

What Kashi soon learned was that the police had been tracking him through a telecommunications device that he was using—Wiremax, a mobile Internet device that is plugged into a USB port to provide mobile connection for the laptop.

The government had access to all of his registered telecommunication devices, and they were able to track him and monitor his activities. Because the state owned the company, no official warrant was needed.

Christians in Iran today are continually subjected to this culture of fear. They know their children are not safe at school. They know that no election is going to change the situation. They know that every telephone call, e-mail, or text message could be monitored. They know that the legal system is not going to save them on the basis of justice and human rights. They know that the moment they begin to follow Jesus, their lives are going to change forever, and although their names are written in the Lamb's Book of Life, they might also be monitored by the local authorities.

Iranian Pastor Haik Hovsepian wrote, "[The Islamic] Revolution has been such a great blessing for the church, because we have learned so many lessons that we otherwise wouldn't have learned. The persecutions helped the elect to remain in Iran and continue the work in spite of all kinds of hostilities from the enemies."

Pastor Haik's words were echoed by one of the most well-known underground house church leaders in China, Pastor Zhang

Rongliang, when he wrote something very similar from the inside
of Xihua Prison:

> *Suffering challenges so many people in the world.*
> *Without suffering how is it possible to taste the depths of*
> *the goodness of the Lord? After tasting of it, how can one*
> *be obsessed with worldly desires?*
>
> *Oh Suffering, I used to flee from you. But today the Lord*
> *has commanded me to endure all that you have for me.*
>
> *Oh Suffering, did the apostles not welcome you?*
> *Suffering invites the seekers to go along with him. He calls*
> *out to me and says, "Come and shake my hand."*
>
> *Oh Suffering, let me embrace you. It tastes good that I*
> *was one with you in the Lord.*
>
> *Oh Suffering, how many disciples have you fed?*
> *Without you, life has lost its struggle. I ask you to visit me.*
> *Let me taste only a bit of the sweetness that you give.*
>
> *Oh Suffering, you make the moments with my Lord so*
> *much better. You are the oxygen of the saints. Without*
> *you, they would have stopped breathing. You are so close*
> *to me.*
>
> *Oh Suffering, let us walk arm-in-arm together.*

The suffering and persecution of Christians at the hands of
Muslims is as old as Islam itself, but Iran has seen a spectacular
display of cruel treatment that has been endorsed by the Supreme
Leader and systematically implemented by the government. There
are more testimonies about those who have suffered persecution in
Iran than can be covered in this book.

If we listen closely to the testimonies of persecution, miracles,
heartache, and triumph, we will again see the book of Acts come
alive and know that the same God who spoke to the leadership in
Iran and used them to take down the Babylonian Empire to set His

people free is poised and ready to do it again in a more mighty way than before.

14

THE UNDERGROUND HOUSE CHURCH

Anyone flying over Iran can see with his or her own eyes that much of the country is arid dry desert. Some of the hottest places on earth can be found in eastern Iran where drug runners risk their lives to smuggle goods across areas that are too hot for human habitation.

Except for the northwestern provinces along the shores of the Caspian Sea, most of Iran only receives six to ten inches of annual precipitation. In any other place on earth, that would result in barren land, devoid of crops and metropolitan areas, but not in Iran.

In some of the most unforgiving terrain on earth, Iran is able to miraculously grow fruits, vegetables, and cotton and provide plenty of fresh water for livestock and sustain large populations. At first glance, it defies the laws of science and rational understanding.

However, the secret to Iran's successful irrigation in the desert plains goes back more than one thousand years before the birth of Christ. An aerial view of Iran or a drive across the country will not reveal to you the secrets. For the answer to this phenomenon you must go underground.

More than three thousand years ago, the Iranians invented a system known as the karez, also known as the qanat, which is a series of underground man-made canals that provide water irrigation. Today, the karez is recognized as a masterpiece of early engineering, and it was copied by civilizations all over the world.

Early Iranian civilizations could live anywhere they wanted as long as they were able to build a system of canals underground. There are conservative estimates that Iran still has twenty-two thousand ancient, underground water canals or aqueducts that go on for more than 170,000 miles and supply 75 percent of all the water used.

The systems are still being studied, because Iranian engineers figured out a concept several thousand years ago that many have forgotten today: simple can be smarter. A system like the Iranian underground aqueducts, with few moving parts, will save time and energy and will be easier to replicate and maintain.

Sometimes tourists driving in Iran see large, tall buildings standing alone. These structures are usually several hundred feet high and are often mistaken as a minaret or Islamic religious tower used for the call to prayer, but they are not. They are actually not religious at all but are used to condition and cool the air in the aqueducts during the hottest part of the day.

The warm desert wind blows into these large towers and flows down into the canal system. Openings at the other end help suck air into the towers, and the speed is propelled by the force of the actual wind blowing. As the air is brought into the canal system, it is quickly cooled by the underground streams of fresh water. The cool air is then carried along the karez to openings of various houses, which allow it to flow out. The karez system brings both water and air conditioning to the residents of the desert sands.

The underground church in Iran is very much the same. Like the ancient karez that brought water to the deserts of Iran, so too is the Living Water flowing underground to the most difficult places. The ancient fathers of Iran dug canals that are still being used today. God is working in Iran like a stream of underground rivers. It is something that can't be seen from the windows of an airplane or from a casual walk through a neighborhood in Tehran.

Western churches are standing by watching helplessly as Christian after Christian is arrested and tortured, but unbeknownst to them and the government is the fact that Christians are bringing Living Water and changing the climate. The Iranian government is putting all their effort into trying to get rid of Christianity in Iran, but they are hastening its growth.

Underground churches do not get their support from the official churches. If official churches are caught providing aid to underground churches, then they would both be shut down.

However, the homes of the saints are providing the platform for growth, the same way they did for the first three hundred years. It should not be forgotten that Christianity was forbidden in most of the known world for the first hundred years. Persecution in Iran is not worse than what the Romans inflicted on the early believers.

Before there were clergy members, state priests, and the backing of empires, Christianity was the religion of a handful of rebels who were considered criminals for their beliefs. Christians met in secret. They met in homes, caves, and even underground in catacombs. Because women were usually the ones in charge at home, they provided the first Christian community bulletin boards for announcements, procedures, and ceremonies.

Like Iran today, most of the early Christians did not have a Christian text or Bible. Written books were a lot more expensive and were hard to come by. The New Testament was not officially compiled until three hundred years after Christ's death and resurrection, so the early church relied on letters and preachers to come and share with them, much like the Iranian church today.

Today, Persian language Bible publishing is illegal in Iran. In 1990, the Bible Society in Iran was shut down. The doors to the legal Iranian churches have been closed. Non-ethnic Iranian church services are tightly controlled and are mainly for ceremonial purposes, like weddings and funerals.

"Sometimes I have people who come to my church and claim to be new Christians. They will ask me for information and supplies," explained one Armenian pastor to me, "but I have to be careful. Oftentimes they are from the government checking up on me to see if I am helping local Iranians or not. If I am, then I will be arrested and my church will be shut down."

Some Christians in Iran might have services in their own communities, but because of the level of secrecy, some of them will travel for long distances to meet with fellowships that are not in their areas but are trustworthy. Often they introduce themselves by first name only, not just for their safety, but for the safety of others as well.

Despite the persecution, the secrecy, and lack of open coordination, underground churches in Iran are growing.

According to page 24 of a 2013 special report provided by the International Campaign for Human Rights in Iran, "The growth of the house church movement has increasingly concerned the Iranian government." In September 2010, during an event honoring Iranian veterans from the Iran-Iraq war, Heydar Moslehi, Minister of Intelligence, told the crowd, "With house churches, the evangelical current yearly takes thousands of individuals to Christianity and baptizes hundreds." In October 2010, Javan Online, a website run by the Iranian Revolutionary Guard Corps, reported, "In recent months, house churches have spread in the city of Mashhad, and reports indicate 200 house churches have been discovered in the city." Javan also noted that the cities of Mashhad, Tehran, Karaj, and Rasht have the highest numbers of house churches.

Ayatollah Seyyed Hashem Hosseini Boshehri, who delivers the Friday sermon in the city of Qom, warned his followers that "today the global arrogance of world powers has invested in a detailed plan that has created a tendency towards Christianity in our country."

The underground church in Iran is not neatly divided into networks with prominent leaders like they are in China's underground church. Defining the underground church in Iran is as messy as trying to define the borders of Palestine within the borders of Israel.

This radical growth of the Christian house church in Iran is seen as a threat to national security. The Supreme Leader stated, "[Iran's enemies] want to diminish the people's faith in Islam and Islam's sanctities. Inside the country, using various means they [want to] shake the foundation of the faith of the people, especially the young generation. From the spread of loose and shameless lifestyles, to the promotion of false mysticism—the fake variety of real [Islamic] mysticism—to the spread [of] Baha'ism, *to the spread of a network of house churches.*"[1]

Contrary to the propaganda spread by the Iranian leadership, the underground churches inside of Iran have not really been started as a coordinated effort. The leadership is rising up indigenously inside of Iran without explanation, usually the result of a dream.

There are two other factors contributing to the growth of underground churches in Iran.

First, urbanization is playing a huge part. Iran follows China in having the fastest growing urban populations. Twenty-seven percent of the population lived in urban areas in the 1950s compared to almost 70 percent today. Because of the close proximity that people are living in, the misery of Islam is common knowledge. Neighbors know that others are also suffering under the current regime. Information is shared from home to home in an expedient and trustworthy manner. When there are individuals who become Christians and experience miracles, information also spreads like wildfire.

Second, women are playing a crucial role in the growth of the underground house church of Iran. Like the church in the first century, churches in Iran are meeting in homes. Traditionally, homes are usually considered to be the domain of the woman. Prior to the legalization of Christianity in Rome, underground house church leadership was largely made up of women. It was not until the church became legal that male clergy members became so prominent and exclusive. The same can be seen in Iran today. With house churches in urban areas being so dependent on the domestic need, Iranian women play a key role in the organization, planning, and leading of the services.

Both of these characteristics of the underground house church of Iran are identical to the underground house church of China. In Iran today, as in China, there are more women who are coming to Christ than men, and they make up the driving force of evangelism.

Prior to the revolution, women had a level of freedom and independence that had rarely been seen in the Middle East. Today, the value of women in society has taken a sharp decline. Women are second-class citizens in Islamic Iran, but the message of the Gospel gives them equal value. This message of the Gospel plays a key role in situations where a woman is suffering from sexual abuse, domestic abuse, or being forced to share her husband with another wife.

Women are turning to the Gospel in huge numbers in Iran and are finding hope and purpose. In Iranian society they are devalued, but in the underground house church, they are a key component.

In a society that is heavily urbanized like Iran is, women and domestic housewives have a natural network of connection and communication.

The story of Maryam Rostampour and Marziyeh Amirizadeh in the book *Captive in Iran* sheds light on the way women are active in the underground church today. They were both involved in delivering Bibles, training materials, and information to Christians until they were arrested and thrown into prison. Some of the Bibles they delivered were printed in China by Back to Jerusalem.

When they were arrested and all of their Christian materials were confiscated, the arresting officers did not find two scared and fragile young women begging for mercy. Instead, they found two Christian soldiers who did not flinch when commanded to deny the name of Jesus.

In 2008, a young mother named Tina Rad was arrested with her husband for running a house church in her home. She was charged with "activities against the holy religion of Islam" for reading the Bible with Muslims in her home in east Tehran. She and her husband were taken to an unknown jail and beaten for four days until she was finally released on a $30,000 USD bail, which was set at $10,000 USD higher than her husband's. "The next time there may also be an apostasy charge if you don't stop with your Jesus," one female guard warned her. Apostasy is cause for execution in Iran.

Tina's face was badly bruised from the beating that she received during interrogation. She was told to provide all of the contacts and names of people who attended the Bible study at her home or she would risk losing custody of her four-year-old daughter. Tina was the focus of the interrogation because she said she saw Jesus appear to her in a dream and eventually led her husband to Christ.

Only ten to fifteen years ago, it was unheard of for a woman in Iran to be arrested for preaching the Gospel, let alone put in jail, but today women are serving prison sentences.

Only ten to fifteen years ago, it was unheard of for Christian men to be given prison sentences lasting more than a year or so, but today the sentencing and punishment are more severe than ever.

Even though the house church meetings are not big, their collective size is growing. According to *The Daily Caller* in 2012, a former Iranian intelligence officer indicated that with a population of just one million in Shiraz alone, the intelligence headquarters had at least thirty thousand secret files on individuals who had converted to Christianity. The number of Christians attending secret underground house church meetings has grown at such a significant rate that Iran has created a secret squad to infiltrate their meetings. This secret squad has been rarely talked about until now.

15

IRAN'S SECRET ARMY

In May 2014, the First Lady of the United States held up a white sign with the bold, black handwritten words, "#Bring Back Our Girls." In April 2014, 274 girls had been kidnapped in Nigeria and sold into sexual slavery. Many of them were Christians and were forced to convert to Islam and then were married off to Muslim men. "In these girls, Barack and I see our own daughters," Mrs. Obama said, referring to Malia, fifteen, and Sasha, twelve. "We see their hopes and their dreams, and we can only imagine the anguish their parents are feeling right now."

The actions of ISIS had been grabbing much of the headlines in 2014, but in Nigeria, there was persecution on an equal level. According to the United Nations, more than 650,000 people have had to flee their homes because of the violence of Muslims against Christians.

A group known as the Boko Haram caught and beheaded Christian men and took Christian women and forced them to convert to Islam before they were given over to be married to Muslim men. Schools, churches, and Christian buildings have been repeatedly attacked and destroyed in Nigeria for the last five years.

A little-known report was highlighted by the *CTC Sentinel*, a journal published by the Combating Terrorism Center at West Point in October 2014 that pointed out a link between the ruling Muslim cleric of Iran and the terrorist activities of Nigeria.

The article stated, "Despite Nigeria's geographic and cultural distance from Iran, there is no region outside of the Middle East where Iran's ideology has a greater impact than in northern Nigeria. Nigeria's pro-Iranian Shia Muslim community was virtually non-existent thirty years ago, but now comprises about 5 percent of Nigeria's 80 million Muslims."

Nigeria is an oil-rich country that has stronger support for Iran's ideology than "any non-Middle Eastern country."

What few people in the world know is that Iran has a secret unit that is actively supporting terrorism around the world, and today they have a strong focus on the underground church.

The issue, however, is what this has to do with the Christians in Iran and why Iranians tolerate it. If the Iranian government is as oppressive as they are accused of being, then why haven't they been overthrown? Why haven't the people simply consolidated their grievances and risen up against the Ayatollah and his cronies and taken the country back?

If the people have not rebelled, are things really that bad? Are Christians so badly hated by the people that normal citizens are willing to stand by and watch thousands of them being persecuted and murdered every year? They have access to Internet. They are not as in the dark as the North Koreans, so why do the Iranian people allow it year after year?

Surely there would have been a leader or two by now who would have had the courage to stand up against the tyranny of the Ayatollah and started another revolution.

The answers to these questions lie in the actions of the Ayatollah after the Revolution. In 1979, one of the first things that Ayatollah Ruhollah Khomeini did to protect his rule and prevent protests against his leadership was to establish the Islamic Revolutionary Guard Corps (IRGC).

It would be wrong to think of the IRGC as a conventional army because it is much more than that. The Revolutionary Guard stands watch over the leaders and the law that was established after the 1979 Revolution. It is a major political, military, and economic force in Iran that has more power than any conventional army in the West.

The Revolutionary Guard is also far more political and ideological than conventional armies. The most powerful clerics in Iran have carefully placed leading members inside of the IRGC, and several mechanisms have been put in place to ensure that the system does not change.

The people of Iran are no match for the highly trained IRGC. The IRGC is trained to respond to military threats abroad, but they are trained and equipped to handle domestic threats as well. The Revolutionary Guard is the center of Iran's hard-line Islamic security enforcement. Since the war with Iraq ended in the 1980s,

The Qods Force Logo

Above the rifle is a Qur'an quotation: "Against them make ready your strength to the utmost of your power..." (Surah 8, An-Anfal, Verse 60). For the Muslim militias, it is the call to prepare a military force to wage war against an enemy.

the Guard has become less conventional and more political. The most elite elements of the IRGC are currently spending more money to effectively control its own population than on protecting its citizens from an outside attack. The main enemy of the IRGC is not an outside army but is increasingly its own citizens.

To handle the ideological challenges both abroad in places like Nigeria and domestically in Iran, the IRGC has created a large intelligence operation and unconventional warfare component called the special Quds Force, which is the equivalent of a special forces division. An accurate force strength of the Quds Force is not available.

The Quds have carried out several terrorist missions against Western and Jewish targets around the world to establish an Iranian revolutionary presence. IEDs in Iraq used against American troops are supplied by Quds. Attacks against Christians in Lebanon are supported by the Quds in Iran.

The Quds' biggest outside proxy is the terrorist organization Hezbollah in Lebanon. They supply the training, arming, and funding of Hezbollah as well as Shia militia and various Taliban activities in Afghanistan.

The exact relationship between the Quds, Hamas, and the Palestinian leadership is more speculative than their known relationship with Hezbollah, but most intelligence communities agree that the Quds are funding hostile Palestinian elements in both the Gaza Strip and the West Bank, although the scale of support is not known.

In short, the Quds special operation force is the long arm of Iran, which for the past three decades has been little more than an exporter of global terrorism.

The U.S. State Department gave a report called Country Reports on Terrorism 2010 that stated, "In 2010, Iran remained the principal supporter of groups implacably opposed to the Middle East peace process. The Quds Force, the external

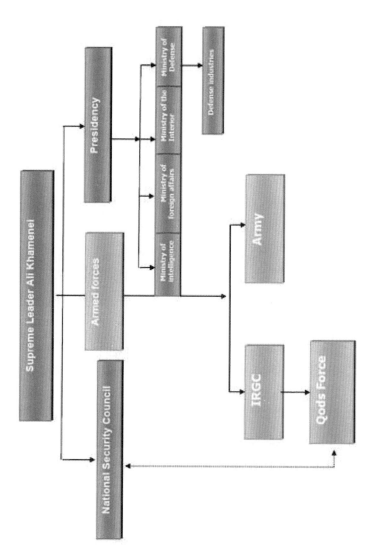

operations branch of the Islamic Revolutionary Guard Corps (IRGC), is the regime's primary mechanism for cultivating and supporting terrorists abroad."[1]

According to a report published in July 2014 by the McKenzie Institute, Iran finds underground house churches to be a growing threat to security. "The Islamic regime of Iran will use any means to impose this idea on Iranian society—that evangelical Christianity and the 'house-church' movement is a deviant form of Christianity and thus is far from true Christian beliefs."

In a report presented to the UN Human Rights Council on March 17, 2014, the UN Special Rapporteur warned that Iran's Christians are still in danger across the country.

Much of the danger is from a secret covert unit within the Quds Force that reports directly to the Supreme Leader. The man heading up this covert unit has been identified as Major General Hamed Abdallahi.

A former Iranian intelligence officer defected to Europe to seek asylum. In an exclusive interview, he told *The Daily Caller* that the clandestine group known as "Unit 400" has been ordered to use "drastic measures to stop them (underground house churches in Iran)—including imprisonment, torture, and the mass burning of Bibles."

Unit 400 is a top secret special ops unit within the elite wing of the Islamic Revolutionary Guard Corps. In the past, it was tasked with international targets and providing material support for foreign militia groups at the direction of the Supreme Leader.

However, because of the domestic security threat of the Christian church in Iran, it seems that Unit 400 has now been engaged, using their resources and skills to infiltrate the Christian underground circles to destroy the movement from the inside.

There are no written directives from the Supreme Leader to Unit 400 to attack the underground house church, but because of the raids that have taken place on house churches in Iran without judicial warrants, it is clear that the intelligence community is directly involved. Unit 400 has been harassing and terrorizing Christians with threatening messages, texts, e-mails, and phone calls. although this seems to be the same as before, it is much different because Unit 400 has the ability to track Christian leaders who now live abroad.

One evening in 2014, I was driving through the Appalachian Mountains in eastern Tennessee with ZZ Abedini, the youngest sister of Pastor Saeed Abedini, who is currently in prison in Iran for being a Christian.

She was on a phone call and said a few words in Farsi, but I could not understand anything.

"Strange," she said as she hung up the phone.

"Why?" I asked out of curiosity.

"I have been getting many phone calls from Iran—from people I do not know, asking who I am and where I am."

It was her US phone number, and only her closest relatives had that number. She had not given it to anyone else. The chances of someone from Iran accidentally stumbling across her number in the United States was zilch.

The phone call ZZ received on her phone was in line with the reports from an Iranian intelligence officer who sought asylum in Europe. "The Guards intelligence (Unit 400) has assigned a unit in major cities, across the country, with the order to infiltrate their (Christian) groups, identifying pastors and the members, then make arrests, forcing them under torture to agree to appear on TV, confessing to criminal activities and having connection with Israel or America," the former intelligence officer reported to *The Daily Caller*.

Another method of interrogating Christians revealed by the former intelligence officer is to bring in the spouse or other loved ones and have them beaten while the Christians watch. Some Christians are kept in total darkness in dungeon-like cells for weeks with no human contact so that the prisoner loses all sense of time.

A Mohabat report indicated that another tactic used at Evin Prison is to bring in the children of the Christian convert and make them explain to their children why they are bringing so much pain on the family.

Unit 400 is well versed in international spying and espionage and can be extremely effective in gaining a foothold into the hundreds of underground Christian services taking place throughout Iran on a daily basis. Using covert Unit 400 on Christians is just another sign that the current regime in Iran sees the growing influence of Christianity as a major threat.

The violence against Christians in Iran is only getting worse, and there are many casualties.

16

THE PERSECUTED OF IRAN

With all the statistics and news reports about Iran's persecution of Christians, it is easy to forget that these are *real* people, with *real* families. It is good to remember the ones we know about like Pastor Saeed, but it is also important to remember that for every story we hear, there are many more that we will never know about.

There are so many stories of hardship and suffering of Christians in Iran. Many of the fallen believers in Iran will never be known by anyone other than the ones they touched on this earth. Many of the soldiers who have sacrificed and given their lives for the Good News of Jesus Christ are nameless and faceless to the rest of the world.

The stories we do know about and the names we are aware of bring us a step closer to understanding the situation in Iran today.

This chapter is dedicated to those who have suffered for their faith in Iran's efforts to erase Christianity from the country. The brothers and sisters in this section deserve all our respect and honor because of their heroic acts in the face of violence and persecution. The brief stories in this section are only a fraction of those who have been arrested and lost their lives because of the Gospel. If I were only to list the names of those who have been arrested and thrown into prison in Iran since 1979 because of their adherence to the Gospel message, that would be an entire book in itself.

In our world today, there are so many bad role models our children look up to as heroes. In this chapter are real heroes whom our children can admire and strive to emulate. These stories inspire us to give more to Christ. Their sacrifices will inspire the next generation to push even harder and go even further. Stories like that of **Pastor Behnam Irani**. Pastor Behnam Irani is married and has two children ages eleven and five. He has been serving as a pastor in Iran since 2002 and was the leader of a small group in Karaj. In October 2014, he was sentenced to six years in prison for leading house church services, which is considered to be a crime against national security.

He has been imprisoned on charges against the state and has been denied proper medical treatment following a major surgery. He is expected to serve a follow-up sentence for apostasy because he converted from Islam.

Even though Pastor Behnam is old and frail because of his health condition, the Intelligence unit of the Republican Guard has been using an extreme method of sleep deprivation to torture him. Family and friends fear that he might not make it out alive if he is not given proper treatment for his health.

On November 25, 2014, Open Doors UK published a letter from Pastor Behnam on their website:

This is Pastor Behnam from Iran. I am serving my 6 year prison sentence, on charges of my belief in Jesus Christ and evangelizing the kingdom of God. It is a great privilege to talk to my beloved family in Jesus.

Many of my cellmates in prison ask me why I am paying such a huge price for my belief in Jesus Christ. They ask me why I don't just deny my belief and go back to my wife and children? I then ask myself: what cost did the Lord pay to save me, and to transfer me from the kingdom of darkness to the kingdom of light? The death of Jesus Christ on the cross, the blood of the Lamb of God!

Yes this is a huge price. Therefore I am also able to prefer prison over being set free. I have decided to keep my faith in our Lord and stay in prison. Jesus said: if you love your life more than me, then you do not deserve me.

I encourage you to understand the value of your faith. We have received salvation for free but remember it was not free. God paid for it. He sacrificed his beloved Son, Jesus Christ. Remember that there is only one way to God and Jesus told us about it:

"I am the way and the truth and the life. No one comes to the Father except through me." John 14:6.

Let Jesus have access to all parts of your life and allow him to be the Lord of your life. Try to become like the Son of God, Jesus Christ, and think and act like Him.

"I have been crucified with Christ and I no longer live, but Christ lives in me. The life I now live in the body, I live by faith in the Son of God, who loved me and gave himself for me." Galatians 2:20.

God bless you. Amen.

Pastor Behnam Irani

Stories like this give us insight to some of the casualties of the Iranian persecution.

There are so many others who are facing the same challenges. People like **Pastor Youcef Nadarkhani,** who is married and is the father of two small children. He first came under fire in 2006 when he attempted to get his Christian church registered. He tried to do things openly and lawfully, and as a result, he was arrested.

In 2009, he made even more enemies when he complained about his children's forceful indoctrination of Islam. He claimed Iran's own law of religious freedom as a defense, but to no avail. He was arrested again. His treatment was a little less cordial each time he was incarcerated.

After being abused, arrested, and imprisoned over and over again, Pastor Youcef hired the services of a lawyer named **Mohammad Ali Dadkhah**. For representing Pastor Youcef, Attorney Dadkhah was also arrested.

He was sentenced to nine years for "acting against national security." In addition to being imprisoned, Dadkhah has been banned from practicing law or teaching at any university in Iran for the next ten years.

Shahram Ghaedi, Heshmat Shafiei, and **Emad Haghi** were arrested in September 2014 when Ghaedi's home was raided by plain-clothes officers. Ghaedi is an actor who played the role of Jesus in Iranian films and was cast as Jesus in other productions.

Neshan Saeedi was at home with his wife and young daughter in the city of Ahvaz in 2010 when plain-clothes officers came busting into his home. They seized his personal belongings, including a computer, CDs containing Christian seminars and teachings, Christian books, Bibles, and even family photo albums.

The entire family was taken to Chaharshir detention center in Ahvaz where they were interrogated for several hours before Saeedi's wife and daughter were finally released. Saeedi's six-year-old daughter was exposed to the entire ordeal and watched both of her parents be accused of being spies and working for Israel.

Saeedi was finally released on a bail of $250,000 after seventy days of solitary confinement. During the entire time, he was held at an unofficial location belonging to the intelligence section of the Revolutionary Guard, and the authorities tried to map out the leadership, pastors, and converts who attended his church. The methods used against Saeedi, his wife, and his daughter had all of the markings of Unit 400.

Ali Golchin was arrested in 2010 for keeping a Bible and leading house churches in various cities including the capital city of Tehran. He was detained, interrogated, tortured, and held in solitary confinement for more than two months. Even after he was released, he was constantly harassed by local authorities. For his safety, he had to flee from Iran.

Pastor Behrouz Sadegh-Khanjani of the Christian network of the Church of Iran and five other members were arrested and put in prison for converting to Christianity. They appealed in 2011, but the sentence was upheld.

Pastor Robert Asseriyan's home was raided in 2013, and he was soon arrested after the doors of the Assemblies of God church were closed by the Intelligence section of the Republican Guard, most likely connected to Unit 400. He was the last pastor of the church before it was forced to close its doors in 2013.

He was interrogated and then sent to Evin Prison, but he was kept in solitary confinement so that the other inmates were not able to meet with him. The church, which is located on Taleghani Avenue, not far from where the American Embassy once stood, was locked up. The following Sunday after the raid, church members traveled to attend the weekly service, only to find a sign that read "Closed for Major Repairs."

The church did not come under attack all at once. First, the Intelligence section of the Republican Guard asked that the church not allow the doors to be open on Friday out of respect for the Islamic holy day. Next, the church was told that all members attending church services must have ID cards approved by the government. Then the guard ordered that participation in the services be limited. Finally, the church was warned against having services in the Persian language.

At the time of its closing, the Assemblies of God had the largest known body of believers worshipping in the Persian language. Many of the employers of those who attended the Assemblies of God church (identified with ID cards) were forced by the government to fire them.

Pastor Matthias Haghnejad was arrested on July 5, 2014, along with two of his friends, **Mohammad Roghangir** and **Suroush Saraie**, for "crimes against God" and faces the death penalty. He was arrested and tried after security police raided his home and confiscated Christian materials.

Pastor Matthias has been arrested before and has already served time in prison from when he was caught in the middle of a prayer service.

The Iranian police know that Sundays and Christian holidays like Easter and Christmas are great times for arrests because that is when Christians who are under surveillance are most likely to be gathered together in one location with other believers.

Mostafa Bordbar was arrested together with a large group of about fifty other Farsi-speaking Christians when fifteen plainclothes officers raided their home in northern Tehran when they were celebrating Christmas together. Mostafa Bordbar had been arrested before for converting to Christianity and attending house church services, so he was already a known convict.

An eight-page report from Mostafa's court session in 2013 defines Christian evangelical activities as coordinated attacks against the Islamic regime of Iran through established organizations holding underground meetings.

Farshid Fathi was also arrested on Christmas Day in 2010. On the third anniversary, 1,100 days of him being in prison, he wrote a Christmas letter to everyone who had been praying for him:

> *God calls us to walk before Him and be blameless, as he said to Abraham. So far, walking before Him is very sweet and so exciting. It is filled with great endurance, afflictions, hardships, calamities, beatings, imprisonments, sleepless nights, hunger, purity, knowledge, patience, kindness, The Holy Spirit, genuine love, truthful speech and the power of God.*

As of Christmas 2014, Farshid Fathi still sits in an Iranian prison.

Ahmad Bazayar, **Faegeh Nasrollahi**, **Mastaneh Rastegari**, **Amir-Hossein Ne'matollahi**, and **Hosseini** were all arrested during a Christmas celebration in 2013 at Mr. Hosseini's house.

The small group was celebrating the birth of Jesus in eastern Tehran when officers raided the home. The police even went next door and searched the neighbor's home as well, then beat the father of the family.

Pastor Vruir Avanessian, who is over sixty years old, was arrested during a raid on a house church meeting celebrating Christmas. Fifty believers were present at the meeting.

Farhad Sabokroh, **Naser Zamen-Dezfuli**, and **Davoud Alijani** were arrested during a Christmas celebration on December 23 in 2011. Farhad was recovering from cataract surgery at the time of the arrest and was purposefully denied the proper medical attention he needed. His wife was arrested as well, but was released when she signed over the deed to their house as bail.

Noorollah Qabitizade was arrested on Christmas Eve in 2010. He was physically and mentally tortured in order to coerce him to sign statements to recant his faith.

Maryam Jalili, **Mitra Zhmati**, and **Farzan Matin**, all former Muslims, were arrested on Christmas Eve in 2009 along with thirteen others during the special service.

Iran has tightened the reins on the Internet. Iran sees bloggers as a huge threat and Christian bloggers as a double threat.

Alireza Ebrahimi is a Christian convert who shared the Good News through blogs. A number of plain-clothes officers from the Iranian Cyber Police raided his home in Gorgan, the capital of Iran's Golestan Province.

The Cyber Police also raided the homes of two of his Christian friends, **Saeed Mirzaei** and **Sadegh Mirzaei**, who were arrested for apostasy and teaching against Islam.

Alireza Ebrahimi, Saeed Mirzaei, and Sadegh Mirzaei were three young men who were using social media to share the Good News of Jesus Christ with their fellow countrymen.

In an interview with one of the domestic news services, Commander Seyyed Kamal Hadiyanfar said, "We will definitely deal with anti-religion websites and weblogs and those who are after creating riots in cyberspace. Any group which targets people's lives or wealth or is using cyberspace to interrupt religious relations and create division among religions will be dealt with."

Mohabat News said that the Iranian Cyber Police, which is known as FTA, was launched on January 23, 2011, and is a special unit and subcategory of the official Iranian Police. FTA in Persian stands for the police of information production and communication. The unit's primary task is to monitor cyber-crimes and monitor closely Iranian bloggers' activities.

Another Christian blogger, **Sattar Beheshti**, was tortured to death. He had been arrested without a warrant by the Iranian Cyber Police on October 30, 2012, for "action against national security through social media activities" and was eventually tortured to death on November 3 in a police detention center.

There are so many well-known cases in Iran that I am not able to mention here, but for a more complete list of Christian prisoners held in prison in Iran, go to

http://www.opendoorsuk.org/news/documents/iran_prisoner_list.pdf.

These people have given their heart to Christ and refuse to turn back. Each one has fewer resources than the many Christians in the Western church. Many of them do not have access to Bibles, they cannot openly attend churches, they cannot drive to a Christian bookstore and buy a worship CD, and as can be seen above, they cannot even attend a simple Christmas gathering to celebrate the birth of Jesus.

The persecuted church in Iran seems to have so little, but they are spiritually rich.

The following is a note from Pastor Fathi, who has spent much of his time in Iran's notorious Evin Prison. He wrote a letter to his father that captures the essence of the saints in prison in Iran. This letter reveals the raw emotion of a saint in prison:

Dear Dad,

Please accept my warmest greetings from the heart of prison in the name of Jesus. It has been a long time since I have been able to hear you. But I sense the fragrance of your prayers as a cool breeze on my heart and it strengthens me from afar. I have gone through difficult days, but more than ever before I have seen myself in the bosom of the Lord, which is full of love. I have had a deep experience of loneliness, but I have never felt alone.

Often I have been sorrowful because of certain things, but I have never been a slave of sadness. Often I have been insulted, humiliated and accused, but I have never doubted my identity in Christ. Some have deserted me, some have fled from me, of course in no way do I pass judgment on them. My Lord has never left me.

I spent 361 days in a locked cell, and I did not see the sunlight for days, but the mercies of the Lord were made new every morning. I have many things to say, but I like to say how much I love you. I miss you, our other brother and my dear aunty. I miss the little ones and their parents. Please give my greetings to my dear uncle. I know that with power and love, he is praying for me and my family.

I probably cannot be with you for a few years. However, your words and exhortations are in the ear of my soul. I hope that at the end I will be able to see you. But if the Father calls me to the eternal abode, please protect and support my family more than before, especially my children who are dearest to my heart.

The narrow way that I am passing through, I see as a cup that my Beloved has given me, and I will drink it to the end, whatever that end might be. What really matters is that I am my Beloved's and my Beloved is mine.

This is possibly the sweetest truth of my life—that I am His and He is mine.

Two of the brothers send you greetings from here. Also, two sisters who are separated from us by a few high walls. I too, am here am continuously praying for you and your loving family. Please convey my greetings to all dear brothers and sisters who have been praying for me and my family and tell them: In our land the fig tree does not blossom, the produce of olive has failed. The flock is cut off from the fold. Yet we rejoice in the Lord and take joy in the God of our salvation. Because neither the walls nor the barbed wires, nor the prison, nor suffering, nor loneliness, nor enemies, nor pain, nor even death separates us from the Lord and each other.

With love and greetings in Christ,
Farshid[1]

Pastor Fathi's letter and story encourage us. Each one of these saints also teaches us many things about the situation in Iran. From their arrests we can learn more about the underground house church in Iran than any census. The clearest picture that anyone can possibly get of the house church today comes from these arrests if we only pause for a moment and observe.

17

A Picture
of the House Church

On December 4, 2011, a top secret American military reconnaissance drone made by Lockheed Martin was captured by Iranian forces. It was a massive public relations nightmare for the American president, who initially denied the Iranian claims.

What made the situation so embarrassing was the claim that the Iranian cyber warfare unit was able to commandeer the aircraft and safely land it.

In 2011, the United States, Britain, and Israel worked hard behind the scenes with their spy agencies to keep Iran out of the select nuclear-weapons-capable club of nations.

Spies, secret aircraft monitoring, and assassination of Iranian scientists were all part of the secret operations to keep nuclear weapons out of the hands of Iranians. Rarely were these efforts made public, until Iran was able to capture the sophisticated, stealthy, and highly classified RQ-170 Sentinel aircraft.

The spy program was an effort of the Central Intelligence Agency (CIA) of the United States. According to reports, the Iranian cyber warfare unit was able to override the CIA's system by jamming both satellite and land-based signals and generating a GPS attack that allowed the Iranians to have essential control over the landing of the drone.

The Iranians immediately went to work to reverse engineer the captured RQ-170 Sentinel stealth aircraft. There were many customers who came to shop for the information that the Iranians held, namely China and Russia.

There is much to be learned from equipment captured from the enemy. The drone contains information about how the Americans plan to spy. The computer chip was full of information about what the CIA was looking for, which revealed the long-term strategy, fears, and anticipation of the enemy.

In May 2014, Iranian state TV showed a copy of the top secret aircraft that the Iranian military was able to build from the unit that they captured.

Like the drone that was captured from the CIA, there is much to be learned and studied from the information we have available from the arrests that continually take place in Iran. There are many Christians who have been able to make it out of prison alive and into the safety of Western countries so they can tell their side of the story. Like the Iranian military that learn tactics and systems by studying captured drones, we can study the underground church in Iran from the persecution taking place in Iran.

Not only do each of these stories from inside the Iranian prisons inspire us, but from these arrests and raids, we can learn a lot about the underground house church in Iran. If we look closely, we can see that all the arrests and raids collectively teach us five main lessons about the underground church in Iran.

1. Raids and arrests continue because the church continues to grow.

The Iranian secret police would not be spending so much time, effort, and resources on these simple underground house church meetings if they did not see them as a threat. Their presence and growth make them a major target.

Every metropolitan city in Iran has house church fellowships. Back to Jerusalem was able to identify house churches in every city to deliver Bibles and Christian material to.

We do not deliver to every house church fellowship. Many fellowships operate completely independent from other fellowships, so we estimate that we are currently only connected to a small fraction of Christian home fellowships in Iran.

However, there is a growing demand for Christian materials that we are not able to meet. At the writing of this book, BTJ had already delivered more than 200,000 Bibles into Iran (including electronic Bibles). Not many organizations are able to smuggle the materials they need into the country, but because of our back-door routes into Iran, we have been able to meet the needs of the believers inside Iran. This has made us (and our materials) very popular with the growing church in Iran, so we have a glimpse of the underground church there.

We know that it is growing, and so does the Iranian government. The increase in raids and arrests that the Christian church is experiencing is also a testimony to this fact.

Most of the raids and arrests are happening to Muslim Background Believers (MBBs), also giving an indication that the newest Christians in Iran are not Assyrian or Armenian believers but are Iranian believers who have converted from Islam to Christianity.

Churches have been closed, publications have been banned, gatherings have been made illegal, and conversions are threatened with death, but the trend continues to go in the opposite direction of the Ayatollah's goals.

The arrests and raids on Christians in Iran today are a big indicator that something is happening. We are able to see a trend indicating growth in the underground house church through the activity of the Iranian crackdowns.

2. The arrests that are taking place rarely take place with large groups. They are always small house church groups.

Like the house churches in China that have experienced one of the strongest growing periods in Christian history, the Iranian churches take place in homes.

The Iranian government sought to destroy the church by tearing down the cathedrals and locking the doors to the sanctuary, but what they failed to realize is that the Church of Jesus Christ does not exist in a building but the hearts of believers. The temple of Jesus Christ is in the followers and is not invested in mortar and stone.

The temple in Jerusalem was destroyed, but the church that Jesus planted continued to grow. Rome spent three hundred years persecuting the followers of Jesus, and not one legal building was built, but the followers continued to grow.

Destroying a building in Tehran will not stop the church in Iran from growing. The small numbers of people arrested during raids tell us that there are only a few people attending house church meetings, but that does not mean that there are only a few Christians.

For security purposes, meeting in homes is ideal for clandestine meetings. The typical home in Iran can only hold a few people at a time, so whenever churches are raided in Iran, the number of people apprehended is often less than twenty.

For Christians used to seeing large mega-churches, it might seem that church meetings of only a handful of people is indicative of only a few Christians, but that is not always the case. Several of the house church networks in China currently have millions of believers. The number of believers in each house church meeting may not be many, but the number of meetings taking place in Iran are multiplying every year.

When it comes to numbers, a few dedicated believers can be very influential. Jesus only had twelve disciples, and only eleven of those went out to share His message after He was crucified, but today it is the world's largest religion.

A quick glance at the number of raids in Iran indicates that the raids are happening in underground house churches, proving that this is where the church is growing.

3. The church growth in Iran is distinctively charismatic.

A 2011 Pew Forum study showed that there are more than 300 million Christians worldwide who are self-identified charismatic. However, due to the lack of transparency in closed countries, the number of Christians who are distinctively charismatic is grossly underestimated.

Since it started in the early 1900s, it is the fastest-spreading form of Christianity in closed countries today, including Iran. Like China, Iran's underground house churches are distinctively charismatic. The charismatic movement in Iran, also known as "Spirit-filled," has been greatly influenced by the Assemblies of God church. A man by the name of Andrew D. Urshan played a very important role.

Andrew was born in Iran in 1884 and immigrated to the United States in 1901, the very year of the revival in Topeka, Kansas, that launched the Pentecostal movement. What took place in Topeka soon spread to Azuza Street in Los Angeles, and a couple of years later, Andrew was baptized in the Holy Spirit in Chicago in 1908.

Six years later, Andrew returned to his homeland of Iran and established a Pentecostal church. Interestingly enough, much of the persecution that Andrew experienced in Iran was from other churches and missionaries. The charismatic movement was viewed with great skepticism by other Christian denominations.

In the *Weekly Evangel*, Andrew recalled when his mother advised him, "Son, be very careful in speaking of the Holy Ghost; don't mention it too much."[1]

In one instance, Andrew recounted how a mob of Eastern Orthodox Christians attacked a group of Pentecostal girls who were headed to church in the town of Urmia. They shot the young girls, hitting three and killing one. Ultimately, though, about fifty people accepted Christ and were baptized in the Holy Spirit in the town of Urmia, helping to establish one of the first official charismatic churches in Iran.

In spite of the persecution and even being thrown in jail,

Andrew told of revivals in five Iranian towns. In each church that Andrew planted, he saw healings and miracles.

In the August 1916 issue of the *Weekly Evangel*, Andrew gave a rare look into the early days of the charismatic church in Iran.

> *The power of God fell on me; I could not help but weep, and as I sang and wept, the Word of God pierced the hearts of the people. Terrible screams were heard; such cries of conviction and confession that the strongholds of Satan seemed shaken to their very foundation by the power of the Holy Ghost. Some of the women had children in their laps. Such conviction seized them that they practically threw them aside, and cried to God for mercy. I do not remember how many were under conviction, but about six received salvation. The meeting would have continued all night if I had allowed it to, but I said to the people, "We must now stop; don't be afraid, you will get what you want." The power fell on those that were saved and they began to shake. The rest went home, crying to God and weeping.*
>
> *These things raised terrible persecution against me. They told me that I had better go home and praise Him for a couple of weeks and that when I returned, I would reap the harvest.*
>
> *After two weeks had elapsed, we went back to the town and this is the song we sang, "Hold the Fort for I am coming." "Hallelujah." As we sang, we marched along the streets.*[2]

Andrew, according to the next newsletter issue on September 2, 1916, was able to plant a third church in Karajaloo Village. The local Christian priests formed mobs and threatened Andrew with death if he ever entered the town.

> *The people heard that we were coming and the mob took clubs and got ready for us. Someone told us to be careful, to go into the house and not in the streets as the mob was drawing near. I answered, "I will die here," and continued to sing. Soon people heard us [singing], and almost the whole town came. Hallelujah! We went in yonder and when I looked upon the people, I saw the mobs standing afar off. We sang and preached. The power of God came upon Jeremiah's wife and she got saved. He was so happy. To make the story short, in three or four weeks, about 40 got their baptism, and I do not know how many people got saved.*

The movement that Andrew started in Iran continues today. From the arrests and raids taking place, we can see that most of the fellowships are distinctively charismatic. Specifically, the impact of the Assemblies of God has been tremendous in Iran.

4. Leadership is always changing.

Anyone documenting the arrests taking place in Iran quickly realizes that the life expectancy of pastors in Iran is much shorter than other professions. Christian leaders do not stay free for long, and effective leaders stay free for an even shorter time.

Currently, the underground church is facing a crisis in leadership because whenever someone on the ground becomes effective in reaching people or training people, they are highly sought after by the hungry new Christians as well as foreign missions groups.

There are so many new believers in Iran who do not have access to Bibles, fellowships, and resources, so when a pastor or evangelist offers these, they are desperately pursued.

Foreign mission groups are not short on people abroad willing to serve Iran, but what they lack are reliable individuals willing or capable of going into Iran.

There is always the dilemma of matching the needs on the ground with the sources abroad. Any leader who can be the link between the two (source and need) is quickly overworked and at some point becomes targeted by the Iranian government.

Once they are highlighted, they are quickly scooped up by the security forces.

When evaluating the arrests and raids in Iran today, the one thing that quickly becomes clear is that the leadership is attacked. This has created a leadership vacuum, because unlike China, these leaders never really go back into society. The majority of them end up dead, in jail, or abroad.

The Iranian government has learned that leaders who are released back into society only continue to cause more trouble, so they make it possible for the leaders to leave the country. They do not actively endorse it, of course, but they willingly look the other way when many Christian leaders leave Iran for Europe or North America.

In China, effective leaders were put in prison, and when they were released, they returned to churches that had doubled or tripled in size, which strengthened their position of leadership. Despite the risks, leaders rarely left China.

Not so in Iran. The leaders have left Iran one after another. It has been a cycle: leaders are covert, seek God, plant churches, preach the Word, and then are scooped up before effective disciples can be trained. Upon release from jail or prison, the leaders find a way to make it to safety in a different country.

Even today, one of the main local representatives who works with BTJ is waiting to see if their refugee paperwork will be accepted by the American government. If they are ever accepted, they will most certainly be on an airplane, leaving Iran for good.

5. Lack of stable leadership has led to a loose connection among other Christians.

Unlike the underground house church networks in China, there doesn't seem to be any strong connection among the different fellowships. The fellowships are loosely connected, making it more difficult for mutual support and fellowship and more difficult to supply resources to.

The underground house church networks in China often formed under the leadership of a leader or a group of closely connected leaders while they served in prison. Upon release, that prison fellowship created bonds and trust that proved effective in church growth. The Iranian church has not had the same experience among their leaders.

What is taking place in the targeting process in Iran is somehow creating a diaspora, or a scattering of Iranians who are fleeing to other countries around the world. The Iranian government has been completely ineffective in stopping the growth of the church. They have inadvertently created a diaspora among the Christian leadership. To know why that is the case, we must first go into the Iranian prison system and see what has sparked the diaspora among the leadership in Iran's underground house church.

18
INSIDE IRAN'S PRISONS

Abbas Sadeghi was held for forty days in the notorious Evin Prison when it was discovered that he had been working with a Christian group known as Elam ministries.

"My life in prison was limited just to interrogations," Sadeghi said. "They were taking me blindfolded to the interrogation room every morning and mocking my belief. They were saying to me that I was foolish to have converted to Christianity. They said they had arrested [Jesus] Christ and that he was in the other cell."

Sadeghi was granted bail, then later sentenced to six years in prison. When he had the opportunity, like many other Christian leaders before him, he fled to the West via Turkey rather than return to Evin Prison.

"I had no choice but to flee Iran," he said.

Evin Prison is known as Evin University, but it's no school—it is one of the most brutal, dark, infamous prisons in the world. Beatings, torture, rape, mock executions, and brutal interrogations are the norm at Evin Prison. Evin Prison has been the grand legacy of the Ayatollahs and their system of rule in Iran.

Fifteen thousand inmates call Evin Prison home, and they unwillingly carry on the four decades of tradition of empty cries and symphonies of screams that are drowned out by hardened guards and swallowed up by drab concrete walls. Evin Prison only has fifteen thousand inmates because speedy mass executions keep the population from going any higher.

The inmates in Evin's little house of horrors are made up of drug smugglers, dealers, killers, thieves, and rapists as well as journalists, intellectuals, political dissidents, and Christians.

Marina Nemat was only a sixteen-year-old student when she was arrested and sent to Evin Prison. She was considered to be a threat to the government, and she remembers the events well. Her memories of the dark days at Evin Prison haunt her to this day.

"When you clear the gates, you are immediately blindfolded and brought underground," Nemat told FoxNews.com. "They take you for interrogation. They take you to a hallway and sit you down. You are there for a long time. If you move or say anything, you are beaten. You must sit perfectly still, while still blindfolded, and you can wait for hours, days or even weeks."

In reality, the goal of interrogators has little to do with getting at the truth.

"They are not looking for information," said Nemat, now an instructor at the University of Toronto and author of *Prisoner of Tehran*, a 2007 book detailing her imprisonment. "What they want is for you to admit that you affected the national security of Iran."

Some prisoners have their bare feet tied to an iron bed and propped up. Then they are lashed with cables and are made to walk for days on their swollen feet before they do it again. This is the most prevalent type of torture because it is explicitly sanctioned by Sharia Law. Being suspended from high ceilings, arms twisted until broken, crushing of hands and fingers by metal presses, insertion of sharp instruments under fingernails, cigarette burns, and submersion under water are all also acceptable. Many prisoners never make it past this phase of the interrogation because they die.

Nemat miraculously survived six months of solitary confinement in Evin's 209 section, where cells didn't have a bed.

"The cells were just large enough to lie down," she said. "When you lay down at night if you stretched out your arms, you could touch the walls. Every day felt like three thousand years."

The most horrifying experience that Nemat remembers was

when she was blindfolded and led out of her cell and down a long corridor. When the blindfold was removed, she was facing a firing squad. They all aimed their weapons at her, and she knew she was going to die any second, until she was snatched up and led away. "He brought me back to my cell," she said. "He told me that I was sentenced to death in court. I told him that I never had a trial and he said, 'Yes you had a trial, you just weren't there.'"

Mock executions are carried out all the time in Evin Prison. They are also a well-known tactic used by Al-Qaeda and ISIS.

Prisoners like Nemat are put through sleep and food deprivation. They are often beaten to the point where they suffer internal bleeding, and then they are deprived of any meaningful medical treatment.

On the morning of July 27, 2008, a total of twenty-nine people were hung in Evin Prison.

Ali Golchin, a Christian believer, reported to the International Campaign for Human Rights in Iran about his time in Evin Prison where he spent eighty-seven days in solitary confinement:

> *The worst type of detention and torture for a person is to place them in solitary confinement. Why? Because the solitary confinement cell is a place where someone experiences extreme [psychological] pressures. It is a place that's 1.5 meters by 2.5 meters with one metal door that only opens for breakfast, lunch, or dinner, or when they want something from you or to take you to interrogation.*
>
> *You are alone the whole time. And when you are interrogated, you hear the worst things that you've heard your whole life from the interrogator.*
>
> *They threaten you with so many things. One day they say, "You're going to be executed." One day they say: "You are going to jail for five years." One day they*

say "You're going to jail for 50 years." One day they say, "We have your father; we've arrested your family." They put pressure on you from every angle and you have no telephone contact with anyone outside the prison, except when the interrogator allows you in their presence with your eyes blindfolded to call your family only to say, "I am fine, I have no problems, everything is good here." You just have to tell them nothing is going on.

The interrogations are long, with repetitive questions, and emotional pressure. They put a piece of paper in front of you and say, "Write this, confess to this act, work with us." You get sick from the food, the polluted air, the dirty bathrooms. Not a place to keep a human being, even if you are a suspect or convict. This is the worst place to live, they give you one blanket and one mat under you on a cold hard floor. In the winter it's so cold, and in the summer, it is so hot. To escape the heat at night, I would soak my clothing and put them on.

Evin Prison is not the only cesspit in Iran where Christians are tortured, but it is the most well known. It is not easy to find a list of all of the prisons in Iran, but I have listed them here to make it easier for reference.

Evin Prison	Tehran	Known for its political prisoner wing and section 209. Nicknamed "Evin University."
Towhid Prison	Tehran	Once operated by the secret SAVAK. Closed in 2000.

Prison 59	Tehran	A known unofficial detention center secretly used by the IRGC. Prisoners are held, interrogated, and tortured here without record of charges. What happens here is "off the record."
Prison 209	Tehran	The secret section of Evin Prison run by the secret service VEVAK. Like Prison 59, this is an unofficial detention facility where prisoners are held without charge, tortured, and interrogated.
Kahrizak Detention Center	Tehran	Main holding center for judicial system in Iran. Holding cells are all located underground, without access to fresh air and toilet facilities. As many as 6,000 deaths occurred inside Kahrizak during the years 2007 and 2008.
Ghezel Hesar Prison	Tehran	Iran's largest prison
Ghezel-ghale Prison	Tehran	
Vakil-Abad (Central) Prison	Mashhad	Location of many secret executions.
Tabriz Prison	East Azerbaijan Province	Executions by stoning are common at this prison.

Sari Central Prison	Sari	Navid Mohebbi, the youngest blogger ever arrested, was held at this prison that is known for drug traffickers.
Rasht Central Prison	Rasht	Inmates are known to be forced to watch fellow inmates executed here.
Rajai Shahr Prison	Gohardasht, Karaj	Also known as Gohardasht Prison or Karaj. This is the prison where political opponents are thrown away to be forgotten about. Pastor Saeed is at this prison, as are members of ISIS.
Dizel Abad Prison	Kermanshah	Known for ruthless beating of inmates who protest treatment.
Adel-abad Prison	Shiraz	Juveniles are known to be imprisoned here, where hangings are routinely carried out in the courtyard. Related to 1985 Iranian prison movie *Boykot*.
Zahedan Prison	Zahedan	Known for regular female hangings.
Plaque 100 Detention Center	Near Shiraz	Intelligence Ministry detention center focused on the war against Christians.

Shiraz Intelligence 100 Detention Center	Near Shiraz	AKA Plaque 100
Karoun Prison	Ahwaz	Holds the most Ahwazi Arab political prisoners in Iran. The section is cramped with only five toilets shared by more than 300 prisoners.
Behnam Prison	Karaji	Also known as Gohardasht Prison. Is regarded as one of Iran's harshest jails because of the many reports of rape, torture, and executions.
Falak-ol-Aflak Castle	Khorramabad	A cultural icon of ancient prison in Iran heritage.
Heshmatiyeh Prison	East Tehran	Known for its political wing that imprisons families for political purposes.
Qasr Prison	Tehran	Closed in 2008 and turned into a museum.
Kermanshah Prison	Kermanshah	Aka Dizel Abad Prison. Known for hanging children for crimes, some of whom have later been proven to be innocent.
Bandar Abbas	Bandar Abbas	Known for group executions by hanging.

The prison system in Iran would be even more crowded today if prisoners were not executed on a regular basis. Iran holds the record for executions. Iran makes up only 1 percent of the world's population but is responsible for 75 percent of the executions. Iran has a death penalty for a wide range of offenses including cursing the prophet Muhammad, drug charges, adultery, incest, rape, fornication, drinking alcohol, sodomy, same-sex conduct between men without penetration, blasphemy, and conversion.

In the first half of 2011, human rights groups estimated that an average of two people a day were being executed in Iran. In February 2014, there were eighteen executions at four different prisons only a few hours apart.

Many deaths occur in the prison before the inmate even gets a trial, and not even children are exempt.

According to the Human Rights Watch, Iran leads the world in executing children. At least twenty-six juvenile executions have been carried out in Iran since 2005 (out of thirty-two worldwide). In July 2008, it was documented that Iran had 130 children sitting on death row, waiting to be executed.

In 2004, Atefah Sahaaleh, a sixteen-year-old school girl, was executed in Iran by hanging.

In late 2007, Makwan Mouludzadeh was hung for a crime that was committed when he was thirteen years old. He was later found innocent.

As bad as the prisons in Iran are, they are even worse when you think of the fact that they are also home to infants and small toddlers. Mothers of infants who are thrown into prison are often incarcerated with their children, subjecting small babies to the same punishment as the prisoners. Many female prisoners who have since departed from Evin Prison in Tehran have testified to the number of infant children in prison with their mothers.

Not only have underground church leaders had to flee from Iran, but there has been a major flight of Iranians from all walks of life. The best and brightest minds from many different fields and disciplines have left. A "brain drain" has taken place, and it has resulted in a desperate situation in Iran.

19

THE DIASPORA

The persecution of Christians and the prison system have been effective tools in driving Iranians out of their homeland, but that is not why Anna (not her real name) left. Anna has not had an easy life, but you would not know it by looking at her. Even with age, there is a softness about her that brings out her real beauty.

Anna left Iran as soon as the new regime took over in 1979 because of her husband's job. Her family became targets of the new Islamic rulers. Today, like millions of other Iranians around the world, she no longer lives in the country of her birth. At the moment, she is not able to go back.

We were on a small island having lunch together. Anna could not speak much English, so she brought a translator with her.

"I had my first baby at the age of seventeen," she began, "but my husband died in a car crash soon after the baby was born. I soon married again and had two more children with my second husband.

One day, soon after the Revolution, my husband came home and said that we needed to leave immediately because the new regime would be looking for us. I was not able to take my children. I could only take the infant who had not yet been weaned. We hired a guy to take us to the Turkish border, but none of us were dressed for the mountain weather between Turkey and Iran."

I could tell that she did not often tell the story, so I remained silent as she sifted through the old memories. They were not easy ones.

"My baby was only a month old, and it was a dangerous journey. My husband was a military man, so he was more adept to handle the harsh conditions. The guide took us on a longer trek than had been anticipated. I was not able to breast feed, and the bottled milk had frozen. The baby began to cry and would not stop. Immediately the guide grabbed his gun and told me that the baby needed to be killed because it posed too much of a security risk. I didn't allow him. I did everything that I could to keep the baby from crying."

She paused as she reflected back on that night in the mountains. "She died," she said simply of the baby.

"My husband said that the wolves could smell the baby and forced me to bury her. I made a small grave for her and buried her in the rocks. As we continued on, something inside of me stirred. Maybe it was my instinct as a mother, but it made me go back to the grave of my baby. When I went back, I dug my baby back up and miraculously she came back to life!"

"Your baby came back to life?" I asked.

"Yes," replied the translator before Anna could even respond. "I was that baby," she said, "Wow!" with Anna looking over her shoulder, smiling.

"We continued on, to Turkey, where we were arrested and thrown into a refugee camp until several months later when we were given asylum in Denmark."

After they arrived in Denmark, Anna's husband had a hard time adjusting to being a refugee in a European country. He started drinking and became extremely abusive toward Anna, beating her on a regular basis, which led to her attempted suicide by drug overdose.

"When I had arrived in Europe, someone gave me a Bible. I never opened the Bible, but I began to pray to the Son of Mary. When I was in need, scared, or when I needed help, I would pray to the Son of Mary and kiss the Bible, and it seemed to answer my prayers. I realized that there was something alive and powerful in the Son of Mary."

Anna was able to escape from her abusive husband, but she was not able to escape from the longing of wanting to return to her home in Iran. One day she decided to travel back to Iran, where she was promptly arrested and incarcerated.

Anna was accused by the Iranian government as being an enemy of the state. "I began to cry out to Jesus. I told Him that I would do anything to have my family back in safety again. I told Him that if He would deliver me and my family out of Iran, then I would know that He was real and I would follow Him forever."

Almost immediately, Anna was released and allowed to travel out of Iran with her children at her side. Right away she joined a church and fervently started serving Jesus. Like many Iranians who were leaving due to persecution in Iran, she started her own business and worked day and night to make it successful. Her small business provided the income needed for her family and put her children through school. She kept her word. She and her family became Christians. Anna has since led more than one thousand Iranians to Christ and has baptized more than three hundred.

Anna's story is just one of many. Few things have had more influence on the church in Iran than the Christian diaspora abroad.

Because of the persecution and the oppression of an Islamic society, an estimated 180,000 to 200,000 Iranians like Anna flee Iran every year. The majority of those who flee from Iran are educated, and many of them make huge contributions to society. The combined worth of Iranians living abroad is estimated to be about 1.5–1.7 trillion USD. In 2000, the Iranian Press Service reported that the Iranian expatriates had invested between $200–400 billion USD in the US, Europe, and China, but almost nothing in Iran.

People coming from the diaspora, once free from the chains of Islam, have unleashed their creativity and impacted the world around them. People like Pierre Morad Omidyar, the founder and chairman of a popular online auction site, or Tehranian-born Dara

Khosrowshahi, president and CEO of the travel website Expedia, or Tehranian-born Omid Kordestani, the chief business officer at Google and previous senior advisor who now serves as the non-executive director at communication giant Vodafone.

Iranian-born Isaac Larian is the CEO of MGA Entertainment, the largest privately owned toy company in the world, and those familiar with CNN may not be aware that the Chief International Correspondent, Christiane Amanpour, was raised in Tehran. Iranian Americans David and Paul Merage co-founded Chef America Inc., where they created the popular Hot Pockets.

What has been a loss for Iran has been a gain for the rest of the world. Iran's best and brightest have made amazing contributions to the rest of the world that Iran desperately needed. Although the host countries in North America and Western Europe have been dealing with many of the problems brought on by liberal migration rules, the problems do not really apply to the migrants from Iran.

Diasporas are rarely homogenous groups, and the Iranian diaspora is no exception. Although there are many ethnicities within Iran and in the diaspora of Iran, by and large, it is still safe to say that Iranians tend to adapt to society, educate their children, and do not burden the host country they immigrate to.

In January 2006, the International Monetary Fund (IMF) found that Iran ranks highest in brain drain among ninety-one developing and developed countries. Most leave because of persecution or lack of opportunities in the Islamic environment. According to a 1999 study, the brain drain from Iran to the United States, measured by migration rates of the individuals with tertiary education, is the highest in Asia. The majority of those leaving are scientific scholars and university graduates. In fact, as many as four out of five of those who recently won awards in various international science Olympiads have chosen to flee from Iran once they have the opportunity to do so.

According to a recent census in the United States, Iranians are among the most highly educated in the country. More than one in four Iranian Americans above the age of twenty-five holds a graduate degree or above, the highest among sixty-seven ethnic groups. The Iranian per capita average income is 50 percent higher than that of the US population.

Many of the Iranians who left Iran looking for freedom immigrated to America. So many Iranians fleeing from Iran settled in Los Angeles that it is often referred to as Tehrangeles. Los Angeles and the rest of the state has such a high number of Iranians that California has a higher number than the next twenty states combined. Today there are twenty television and five radio stations broadcasting in Persian from Los Angeles to Iranians in the United States and Western Europe, and even to Iran, although such broadcasts in Iran's Islamic Republic are illegal.

Iranian Christian programs, which are forbidden by the Islamic state, are exported from California and Texas to Iranians in other countries and even smuggled or broadcasted into Iran itself. Most Iranians who leave Iran desire to go to America. Although the mullahs hide it, their country is full of citizens who love America. It is often called the most pro-American country of all the Muslim countries in the world.

A 1998 census shows a rough breakdown of Iranians in America.

Southern California	550,000
Northern California	200,000
Washington, DC	120,000
Texas	100,000
New York	80,000
Chicago	20,000
Other Areas	280,000
Total	1,350,000

It is important to note that many Iranians who fled Iran did not consider their departure permanent. They were very much like the Shah who fled in 1979. They expected to return. Many locked up their homes, packed a few suitcases, and viewed leaving as a temporary sojourn from their lives in Iran, which would resume when the revolutionary government was overturned. However, as time goes on, the possibility of a permanent return seems increasingly unlikely.

Unfortunately for the Islamic regime, most of the refugees fleeing Iran are highly skilled individuals leaving universities and research institutions.

The *Iran Times* estimated that one out of every three physicians and dentists (at least five thousand) left after the Revolution. In addition to the reduction in manpower, studies estimate that the flight of capital from Iran shortly before and after the revolution is in the range of $30 to 40 billion.

Recently, most of the asylum seekers fleeing Iran are Christian converts and their families who are threatened with death for acts of apostasy. In 2004, 10 percent of all UK asylum seekers were from Iran. In 2001, the UK alone experienced a 300 percent increase in the number of Iranians seeking asylum in Britain.

Many of these Iranians who have fled to Western countries are leaders in their fields of study. This is also true of the church. Many Christian leaders in the church have been forced to leave and now reside outside of Iran. Many of these believers did not want to leave Iran and even today stay very close to their Iranian communities, but in order to survive, they now live in the West.

However, their hearts remain heavy for the persecuted church in their home country, and that has motivated them to launch initiatives in Iran.

20
Supporting the Underground Church in Iran from Abroad

It was only a small office on the outskirts of London. The glass door to the entrance was closed and without a code. It was not possible to get in. The building seemed rather secure for such a remote area. Brother Ren and I had traveled to the UK together with Brother Yun to raise the awareness of the Chinese Back to Jerusalem missionaries and were now at the suburban headquarters of Pars Theological Centre. Pars had to be careful with security because of their illegal work in Iran.

The explosive growth rate of the Iranian underground church has led to the formation of many small groups throughout the country, but because of few resources and lack of leadership, there is a real danger of heretical teachings.

Many Iranians who are a part of the underground house church are at different stages on their journey to know more about Christ. Some have only had an experience, like a dream or a vision, but have very little knowledge about following Christ. Others have been exposed to other Christians and Christian material and know a little more.

Anyone who has access to the Bible or Christian teaching can quickly become a de facto pastor. Young Christians are quickly thrown into the furnace of leadership to meet the demands of a growing church. Solid theological teaching is essential to continued healthy growth, and groups like Pars are helping meet that demand.

From the moment we walked into their office, we were met right away by administrative staff who were busy enrolling students, preparing more training materials, and registering classes. With their intense schedule, it would have been understandable for the staff to say a friendly hello, introduce themselves, shake hands, and go back to tackling the important tasks of the day, but hospitality is in their Persian blood. Even though we were in England, the Pars Theological Center still exhibited the Persian culture, where we were kindly served tea, cookies, and chocolates that had been flown in from Iran.

Dr. Mehrdad Fatehi came into the room and welcomed us to his center. His warm, gentle presence quickly puts everyone at ease. His salt-and-pepper-colored beard adds to his grandfatherly demeanor. He also carries an intellectual aura about him. As I shook his hand and said hello, I found it hard to imagine that this man would be a criminal in Iran.

Dr. Mehrdad is one of the main personalities preparing the ground for even greater revivals in Iran. I first learned about him from Dr. Sasan Tavasoli and Rev. Tat Stewart during a small "By Invitation Only" Iranian conference in Los Angeles. I also recognized his face from the programs that he is in on SAT-7 Pars, which is a satellite broadcast that targets Farsi-speaking audiences in Iran, Afghanistan, Tajikistan, and the diaspora in Europe.

So many believers in Iran depend on broadcasts from SAT-7 Pars and Pars Theological Centre for biblical teaching. They also have nowhere else to turn to when facing issues affecting them today.

Dr. Mehrdad and his team outside of London are a part of the Iranian diaspora who are making an impact on their home country even though they are no longer living there. They are intimately familiar with the needs and have developed discipleship programs to assist the growing underground church.

Pars Theology Centre provides seminary training for students who enroll in their courses. Pars is constantly looking for ways to enroll their students, train them, grade them, and even certify them through a system of underground networks. They use materials that are carried in by hand and given to the students. They use satellite broadcasts that the students can find through satellite dishes and VPN-assisted Internet connections as well as small microchip devises that can be hidden in the smallest of places and swallowed if necessary.

Through this network, Dr. Mehrdad and his team are able to connect with their students in Iran and provide a formal education so they can obtain a certified and internationally recognized bachelor of arts (BA) degree in theology.

"Take a look at this," Dr. Mehrdad said as a full-course outline was given to me. I was reminded of my own days in the seminary when I was required to take the exact same courses.

Pars Theological seminary uses a chain of theological seminaries around the world to provide on-line study, intensive teaching conferences, and host video conferencing seminars. It is one of the most comprehensive courses available in any closed country in the world today.

Pars is not the only group in the world doing this. Many of the Iranian Christians who have fled from the persecution in Iran are now working on initiatives to help get the Gospel into Iran and help train disciples.

The power of communication made possible by modern technology is assisting in this effort in ways that have never been possible before. We at Back to Jerusalem are taking advantage of this modern technology as much as possible.

Anna is helping head up the discipleship program implemented by the Chinese who are going to Iran as missionaries. Anna has led more than one thousand Iranians to Jesus Christ and is using her experience and passion to help the Chinese.

Anna's team has translated the entire Chinese children's Sunday school training program known as DOVE into Farsi. DOVE has been used in China to train more than 25,000 Sunday school teacher trainers who have, in turn, trained more than 250,000 Sunday school teachers throughout China. It is the only complete Sunday school training curriculum that has been completely compiled and developed by Chinese Christians *for* Chinese Christians. Because of the success of DOVE in the underground house churches of China where evangelism to children under the age of eighteen is illegal, it has also been used in other countries like Vietnam, Ethiopia, Mongolia, Pakistan, India, and even in more open countries like Norway, Sweden, Lithuania, and Finland.

The Back to Jerusalem DOVE training program used by the Chinese is unique in that it does not merely focus on teaching Bible stories to a passive child, but it encourages and motivates the child to be used by God. The child is not only a recipient of the Gospel message but becomes a conduit for the Gospel message to be spread to others.

"This is a huge need in the Iranian church," Anna said in January 2015. "Children's programs are currently our largest need, and I really love what the Chinese have done with the DOVE program."

Because of the persecution in Iran, children are sometimes forgotten, but they are the future of the church. The Iranian government has not forgotten them or left them behind. They focus their radical Islamic agendas and ideology on the schools so that children of the youngest age start their understanding of the Islamic Revolution early.

Anna is also assisting the Chinese with their Persian language studies by providing teachers who diligently take the time to teach their mother tongue to the Chinese prior to them moving to Iran. With the number of Chinese moving to Iran increasing, so is the need for language teachers.

Even though people like Anna and Dr. Mehrdad would be considered criminals in Iran, they are heroes of the faith to Christians around the world for sacrificing so much of themselves for the Gospel.

"So many times I have Iranians who come to me and ask questions about Jesus," Anna told me during a lunch in January 2015. "They do not know anything about Jesus except for what the Koran says and what the government tells them, but they want to know more. They are curious and hungry." Anna knows what it is like to be Iranian and to be without hope. She also speaks from experience when she shares with Iranians who grew up learning Shia Islam but who are curious about Jesus.

The Iranian diaspora has brought about a sizeable number of Iranians who are now providing resistance to the Iranian regime from the outside. These same Iranians are also providing resources and encouragement to the growing church inside.

Just because Anna and Dr. Mehrdad live outside of Iran is no guarantee of their safety, which is just one reason why Pars Theological Centre is in a secure building outside of London.

On Valentine's Day in 1989, Ayatollah Khomeini sent out a love message for Muhammad and commanded all Muslims to seek out and kill Sir Salman Rushdie, who wrote about *The Satanic Verses* of the Koran in his novel. The Iranian leaders have been the most radical in hunting down Sir Salman Rushdie, even offering a reward for his death. Sir Rushdie did not live in Iran, but it did not stop the Iranian government from calling for his death.

In 2012, Iran raised the bounty on Sir Salman's head, from $500,000 to $3.3 million USD. During Friday prayers in February 2014, Senior Iranian Cleric Ahmad Khatami told worshippers that Sir Rushdie's fatwa, or death warrant, is as "fresh as ever."

Anna, Dr. Mehrdad, and the thousands of other Iranian Christians living outside of Iran are constantly reminded that they are never really safe from the reach of the Iranian government.

21
REACHING IRAN

With all the efforts Iran has taken to keep Christianity out, it has not succeeded. There are discipleship trainings that are taking place on a regular basis with Iranians who are able to travel to Turkey as well as Armenia. These schools are usually short term, but they have a strong focus on training up underground house church leaders.

Elam Ministries is one of the Iranian ministries that actively capitalizes on the vulnerabilities of the Iranian border. They claim to be supporting "church planters, evangelists, and pastors who are serving in more than 70 cities in Iran and the wider region." Many of those leaders receive the Elam training in Turkey.

Groups like Youth With a Mission (YWAM) and 222 Ministries that also have a major focus on Iran choose training grounds like Armenia from time to time to help leaders who are able to get out of the country.

Azerbaijan, Armenia, and Turkey have been major routes for materials and Bibles into Iran. The guards in Armenia are all too aware of their strategic location for ministry to Iran. Georgia has opened up and is much easier to bring Bibles to these days, but those Bibles that make it to Georgia often get confiscated at the border crossing into Armenia.

The Turkish government is also very aware of the activities that are taking place in their country. "We are a legal Bible society here in Turkey and are allowed to import Bibles in the Persian language," said Tamar Karasu of the Bible Society in Turkey during our meeting in Istanbul in March 2012, "but Turkey roughly knows how many Persian-speaking Christians there are and a large number of Bibles would raise suspicion right away."

Prior to 2014, Afghanistan, Pakistan, and even Iraq were used to take Bibles into Iran. I am certain that Turkmenistan has served a role in getting Christian materials into Iran, but I have never been exposed to operations on that side of the border.

Back to Jerusalem has been using these areas as well. Every year BTJ runs projects pertaining to missionary training, Bible printing, distribution of training materials, and even disaster relief for Iranian border regions.

Some of the projects cannot be mentioned because they would be easily identifiable to local authorities and would immediately highlight the work of the Chinese missionaries. It is, however, safe to say that the Iranians have found a partner in China.

Today, because of the huge need for Persian Bibles and biblical teachings in Iran, BTJ focuses on smuggling operations. Every year we have an opportunity to get as many as ten thousand Bibles and teaching materials, including audio/video devices, into Iran.

We have been printing Iranian Bibles in China and sending them to predesignated distribution points along the border of Iran, and during one of the most important holidays in the Iranian calendar, we participate in a distribution blitz.

The Iranian New Year is the largest and most important holiday of the year. It is like the Chinese New Year or like Christmas to Christians. BTJ uses this holiday to specifically target Iranians as they travel abroad. It has been a smashing success!

BTJ targets the Iranian New Year tourists going into other countries because that is one of the most unique times of the year to have the greatest access to Iranians without the scrutiny of the Iranian government. At many borders, the Iranian government is running on a skeleton staff and are not able to check returning passengers as well as they would during other times of the year.

Because of the restrictions imposed on Iranian passport holders, Iranians are restricted from going to many other countries in Europe or to America or Australia, so they are forced to go where it is easier for them to get access, like Dubai, Turkey, Armenia, or Azerbaijan. Even though they are restricted from traveling to other countries, they still make an effort to do something special together with their families to celebrate the New Year, and we wait on them to add to their special moment.

To imagine Iranians during Iranian New Year, try to imagine spring break in the West. During spring break, the roads are often packed with cars and buses making their way to popular destinations. Airports and airline companies struggle to meet demand.

Most Iranians are tired of the oppressive laws of Iran, and many of them feel they are held hostage by the religious leadership and are quite frankly sick of Islam and need a vacation away from it. The overwhelming desire to go somewhere new and exciting makes them open to opportunities for sharing the Gospel with them.

Because there are so many families, there are also rare opportunities to reach children. We are able to hand out many children's Bibles that tell the Gospel message through pictures. When BTJ has handed out these children's Bibles, we have rarely seen them turned away. In fact, they are excited about receiving them. Some parents who saw free children's Bibles being handed out immediately sent their children over to receive one. Little children would run up to our team and kindly ask for one. Once they were able to get one in their hands, they would grip it tight, hold it to their chest, and run excitedly back to their families. Fathers can often be seen sitting around the distribution area reading the new Bible that their children had just received.

Iranian New Year is also a time when we see many Iranians become Christians. Sometimes BTJ is assisted by ethnic Iranians who are able to share about Jesus in the Farsi language. Teenagers and young adults are especially open to the Good News. Young Iranian women step off of the buses from Iran and let their hair down. Their desire to be free to wear what they want makes them obvious Iranian tourists. They yearn for the freedom to make their own decisions about what they must and mustn't wear.

In March 2014, during Iranian New Year, there was an older woman who was in her late fifties or early sixties. She was short and stout and did not particularly stand out from the other tourists who had just arrived from Iran. Soon after she stepped off the bus, she was handed a Bible for the very first time. She left Iran only expecting to have a vacation with her family. When she was presented with a Bible, her face was filled with shock.

She pressed the Bible up to her lips and kissed it. Then she held the book up to her scarf-covered forehead, closed her eyes, and began to weep. She had been secretly praying for a Bible and did not know when or how God would answer her prayers. The book she was holding in her hands would make her a criminal when she returned home, but in that brief moment, as she stood in front of the BTJ workers, she was a free woman who had just had her prayers answered.

For many Iranians, receiving a Bible is an answer to prayers. For others, however, it can be a nightmare. Even though the borders are loosely guarded during Iranian New Year, fear is used to make up for the lack of personnel.

"Does everyone on this bus see this book?" the border guards will ask according to one Iranian Christian I met with in Turkey. The customs officers at the Iranian border will board the buses and hold up a copy of the Bible in their hand for everyone to see. "This book that I hold in my hand is illegal. If you were given this book while you were abroad, or found it in your hotel or on the ground, it is illegal. If you pull it out now and give it to me or one of my colleagues, you will not get in trouble. However, if we search this bus and find one in your luggage or on your person, then you will be taken off this bus and arrested."

It works almost every time. You can see people pulling small Bibles out of their suitcases and backpacks and handing them to the customs officials. For those who do not know what being a Christian is all about, it is not a chance they are willing to take.

Those who have been across the border from Iran before know the challenges they face when they head back. Even though some of them would really love to have a Bible to take back with them, they know it is possible they will get caught with it and be put in prison. So for those who were concerned about breaking the law and getting caught, we were able to provide a solution for them.

Almost everything that is produced in the world today carries the label "Made in China." China is the birthplace for many of the world's electronics, including microchips. We have been able to produce tens of thousands of small microchips that are smaller than the smallest coin. These small microchips, also known as micro SD chips, are useful; they can easily get past the customs officers.

We are able to fit the entire Bible, discipleship training, music, and videos on these small microchips and hand them out to the Iranian tourists while they are on vacation. Many of the tourists find the microchips to be fascinating and will put them into their mobile phones to see what is on them.

One of the things that makes these materials so special is that they are in the Persian language. Never underestimate the power of the mother tongue. The Koran is mainly available in Arabic. Other languages are discouraged and often forbidden. The Koran can never reach the heart of the Iranian because it is not in their heart language. That is why we try to provide all our materials in the language of the people.

Not only are we handing these items to Iranians on vacation, but BTJ is now producing them in China and smuggling them into Iran. We are also copying the material and distributing them in Iran. It is one of the most dangerous projects we have been involved in thus far, but it is paying off.

22
BTJ's Secret Operation Inside Iran

Working with the diaspora outside of Iran is one way of getting the Gospel message into Iran, but it is limited. To really reach the underground house church, it is absolutely essential to work from the inside. The majority of the population in Iran are young people who are still living at home and are not yet able to travel abroad. If efforts are not made inside of Iran, only a small fraction of them will ever be reached.

Today, the majority of the population are young people under the age of thirty. When the Ayatollah took over in 1979, all forms of contraception were banned. This led to a baby boom. Realizing that they had made a mistake, they later dropped the ban, but it was too late.

Today, Iran has the only condom factory in the Middle East, and if a couple wants to marry, they must first take an hour-long seminar on contraception. Iran has been trying to curb the radical growth they have been experiencing.

Besides the increase in population from banned contraception, there was also a huge jump in babies born illegitimately outside of marriage.

The US State Department cites Iran along with the Democratic Republic of Congo, North Korea, and Saudi Arabia as hubs of human trafficking. Young girls are sexually abused. It is often the girl who suffers the consequences of adultery laws in Iran instead of the traffickers when she is caught with a child.

174 Jesus in Iran

In recent years, child prostitution has risen 635 percent in Iran. In Tehran alone, an estimated eighty-four thousand women and girls are in prostitution. This abuse is usually made possible because of the loose laws surrounding *sigheh*, or short-term marriages, which are permitted under Sharia Law. These marriages are not real marriages but are the legalization of prostitution as they only last from one hour to several months. These sigheh marriages are used to satiate the sexual desires of abusers without the stigma of adultery.

Runaway girls and young ladies who have been trafficked are often subjected to become an extra wife to make money or gain their freedom. A man can have several sighehs within a twenty-four-hour period if he wished.

A man can take a young girl to a mullah and ask to be married. Before the ceremony begins, tea is often presented and negotiations of time and payment are agreed upon between the man and the woman. Anyone witnessing it can plainly see that it is legal prostitution. The man can agree to pay a certain price to be with a lady for a certain period of time. Once the agreement is made, then the mullah can pronounce them to be married. This is usually done in a back room with no ceremony.

Although pedophilia is allowed, homosexual relationships are banned in Iran. Although not his intention, the former Iranian president had the crowd laughing during a speech at Columbia University in America. "In Iran we don't have homosexuals like in your country," he said in response to a question about persecution against gays. "In Iran we do not have this phenomenon. I do not know who has told you we have it."

Since 2008, Iran has conducted more sex-change operations than any other country in the world except for Thailand.

Polygamy is legal in Iran, and men can marry up to four wives. Once married, a girl can no longer go to high school. The marriage age of girls is currently thirteen, up from nine years old in 1980. Boys can marry at the age of fifteen, the legal age that Iranians can vote. Polygamy is also a contributor to the increase in population. With the large number of young people who are not able to leave Iran, the only way to reach them is to go inside the country, and that is what BTJ is doing.

***

Besides handing microchips to Iranians on vacation in other countries, BTJ is also providing them to the Iranians inside the country by the thousands. The microchips or micro SD cards that are provided by BTJ inside of Iran are made at places inside the country that we call Bread Factories.

The Bread Factories do not provide loaves of bread made of yeast and flour, but instead they provide the Bread of Life.

After successfully getting "ovens" into the country, we then place them in strategic areas throughout the interior of Iran, and those locations become our Bread Factories. In 2014, we were able to deliver several thousand units that contained the Bread of Life throughout the country of Iran.

BTJ has purchased vehicles that are able to take the Bread of Life from the factories to the various locations and underground house church groups throughout Iran.

The micro SD chips are placed in a universal chip that allows the chip to be used in mobile phones, tablets, computers, e-readers, etc. The micro SD card is put into a larger SD card that can be read by any device that can read SD chips. The side of the card that is produced and shipped in from China has a removable edge so that it can be read by any device that uses USB. That means that BTJ is distributing chips that can be used as micro-SD chips, standard SD chips, or USB.

These three electronic adaptations (SD card, micro SD card, and USB in one) make it possible for the content to be accessible to almost anyone with a mobile communication device. This USB/ SD/micro SD adaptation can be used with computers, phones, or tablets to listen and watch or read the content provided. All of the content is specifically tailored for Iranians.

"We need at least a million Bibles in Iran," Brother Ren told me in early 2012 before we set up our first Bread Factory. Brother Ren is the director of the Back to Jerusalem movement internationally and also the acting pastor for Brother Yun.

"Is that possible?" I asked. I had never even heard of a million Christians in Iran. How would it even be possible that a million Bibles are needed there?

"I had a secret meeting in Tehran with one of the top underground house church leaders who helps deliver Bibles in Iran," Brother Ren continued, "and he told me that they have an immediate need for Bibles—a million Bibles."

I was amazed. If what that leader told Brother Ren was even remotely true, then that would mean the international estimation of the number of Christians in Iran is wrong.

Brother Ren and I began to work to get duplicators that are specifically made for mass copying of micro SD cards and smuggle them into the country. These duplicators are like ovens that bake the micro SD card for the Bread of Life. We have a master unit that has the Iranian Bible, music, videos, and discipleship teaching that we use to copy all the micro SD cards.

As amazing as the Bread Factories are in Iran, few things are as exciting as what BTJ is doing with their new unit called the Gospel Cloud.

China is the place where so many things are made, so all of the materials needed for new ideas are readily accessible. When we needed something a little more technologically advanced that did not yet exist on the market, we decided to make it ourselves.

In 2014, we were able to invent a secret device called the Gospel Cloud. The Gospel Cloud unit is designed to enable the distribution of digital material in areas with restricted or no Internet access, even off the grid. The specific design allows for unique and clandestine one-on-one evangelism in places where proselytizing is illegal.

The Gospel Cloud is a handheld electronic device that is about the size of a mobile phone. It is battery powered and sends out a Wi-Fi signal of about one hundred meters. For security reasons we cannot describe its shape or how it looks, but it is able to deliver simple Gospel tracts, books, news articles, Bibles, commentaries, apologetic writings, and even entire theological studies through Wi-Fi connections. Christian music and movies can be made available for the first time in multiple languages and downloaded at the press of a button. The material can be downloaded in a matter of seconds in a safe and discreet manner.

The Gospel Cloud is designed to be safe and secure for users. No logins are required, and no user data is stored. The system is not connected to the Internet in order to prevent restrictions, bypass government firewalls, and preserve user privacy.

The Gospel Cloud can be used anywhere, at any time, and does not need a power source. Anyone with a mobile phone, laptop, or tablet can connect to the Gospel Cloud using Wi-Fi. It can be used to target people in Iran waiting at a bus stop, hanging out at a café, eating at a food court, or waiting in line at a movie theater.

The Gospel Cloud can even be used at a mosque during prayers when many Muslims play on their phones instead of pray.

Imagine this: An Iranian man sits down at a bus stop and opens up his phone as he is waiting for his bus. He sees that there is free Wi-Fi available in the area that is not secure and doesn't require a password, so he connects. When he opens up his web browser, he immediately sees free music downloads, video downloads, news articles, etc.

He tries to type in a different address like www.google.com or www.news.com, but instead of going to those websites, he is only taken back to a home page that we have created.

The Gospel Cloud is not actually connected to the Internet at all. It is its own server, meaning that the mobile device acts as its own type of intranet, but the man at the Iranian bus stop does not know that. He thinks that he is on the world wide web, when actually he is only connected to our device.

A message pops up on his browser and asks him if he would like to chat or learn more about a product, idea, event, etc. Suddenly the man at the bus stop in Iran with nothing to do is engaged with unlimited resources available to him and the entire experience is completely controlled by the Gospel Cloud.

Local missionaries are now able to chat without revealing who they are. The person waiting for the bus and the missionary can talk using their wireless devices without ever looking each other in the eye, which is important for security in many countries.

The Iranian can download a Bible in less than three minutes and read it as he travels to his next destination. The *Jesus Film* can be downloaded in only a couple of minutes and watched at a later time. If the police catch him and ask him where he got the illegal Christian material that is now on his mobile device, he can honestly say, "I don't know." All he knows is that he simply saw information pop up on his mobile device as he waited at a random bus stop. But he has the Gospel shared with him without risking the security of himself or his family.

Imagine this: Young Iranians are traveling every day by subway. While they wait on the subway they have nothing better to do than fiddle around with their wireless devices. They would have downloaded something interesting before they left home, but they didn't have time. Once they get on the train, they see that the train actually has free Wi-Fi. However, that Wi-Fi is connected to the Gospel Cloud, not the Internet. A missionary on the train with the Gospel Cloud is able to have access to several hundred people all at one time on the subway. The missionary can deliver tracts, Bibles, music, and videos without ever carrying one single piece of paper. Since everything is anonymous, female missionaries are now able to share the Gospel message with men.

I put the Gospel Cloud in my pocket while traveling in Iran. I went to a crowded shopping center and sat down at a coffee shop close to the railing on a high floor overlooking the shoppers. I secretly turned on the device and watched as people all around me connected to the Gospel Cloud.

The Bread Factories and the Gospel Cloud are just two ways that the Chinese BTJ missionaries are able to bring the Gospel directly into Iran to share the love of Jesus Christ.

23

BUSINESS AS
MISSION IN IRAN

Besides setting up Bread Factories and distributing illegal Gospel material in Iran, Chinese missionaries are also focusing on doing what they do best in difficult areas—starting small businesses.

Unlike the Western Christian mission model that is supported by continual funding from the sending church body, the Chinese are going to the mission field in Iran with very little financial support.

In order to survive on the mission field in Iran, they must work in the same manner as the first-century missionaries did for the first three hundred years. They must become "tent makers" (Acts 18:3).

The Chinese church has understood that long-term missions in Iran cannot be done without the sustainability of a skill and trade. In order to multiply and send as many missionaries as possible, China has adopted a business model in Iran that allows them to connect with local Iranians. Their business-as-mission model is very unique and provides a natural inroad into a community to share the Good News.

Business as Mission, or BAM, has emerged as a significant new model for missions around the world. It is quickly becoming the "Coca Cola" of Christian terminology in mission conferences.

Today's globalized economy has created strategic opportunities for Christian businesses in some of the most unlikely corners of the world, including Iran.

Business as Mission (BAM) is a relatively new term but is based on biblical concepts. Other expressions often used include "transformational business," "tent making," "great commission companies," and "kingdom business." These are very generic terms, but the way it is used among the Chinese, in the BTJ context, is different from the way it is usually used by the Western church, and it is important to clarify the differences.

BAM, as it is used and taught today in mainstream Christian curriculum, is businesses with a ministry component. Business and missions are kept separate. BAM is a means to an end in the BTJ vision; mission work is the primary focus and the business is second. Everything done is driven by the primary vision of sharing the Gospel of Jesus Christ, including businesses. The dichotomy between sacred and secular does not exist in BTJ's BAM. The BTJ missionaries do not share the idea that religion and faith need to be quarantined from other aspects of secular life. If we look in the Bible, we see amazing examples of businessmen, kings, leaders, judges, crop owners, and soldiers who interconnected every aspect of their life with the will of the Father.

BAM is a part of a wider global movement in the Chinese underground house church, that is recognizing and responding to God's call to take the Gospel of Jesus Christ to the whole world, even to those parts that don't want it.

To get an idea of the international or mainstream Christian view of BAM and how it is different from the underground Chinese view, a sixty-page report from the Lausanne Conference in Cape Town, South Africa in 2010 said, "Unfortunately there is sometimes a confusing misuse of the term BAM. Let's be clear: BAM is not 'Business for Mission,' a fundraising activity facilitated by the profits generated by business. Neither is BAM 'Business as Platform' i.e. an attempt to obtain visas to do 'real ministry.' Rather, genuine BAM is the practice of business as a calling and ministry in its own right, a manifestation of the Kingdom of God."

Respected academic religious institutions have embraced BAM as it is defined by the Lausanne Conference. However, it is self-admitting that BAM as it is taught and defined by the Western world has a hard time in countries like Iran because "one of the biggest hurdles for BAM businesses around the world, especially in and around the so-called '10/40 Window,' is securing investment capital. BAM is not built on traditional models of charitable fundraising and donations, but on a foundation of the disciplined allocation and return of capital. One of the biggest challenges for the global BAM movement is the lack of BAM investment funds— capital managed with vision, professionalism, excellence and integrity."

It is hard to garner investors in Iran because the business environment does not promise much return on investment. A business would need a stable environment, a functional government, investment security, etc., in order to create a probable model to predict future growth and profits.

Iran cannot provide that kind of stable environment because of their provocative international policies. A business plan for Iran will sometimes last for less than a week because the business climate and government there are so volatile. This scares investors who would like to make as much return on their investment as possible.

For the BTJ Chinese missionaries who are doing business in Iran, BAM is any use of business that advances the Gospel of Jesus Christ in a long-term, sustainable way.

BTJ BAM is not a term created from years of research, study, and analysis. It is a practical endeavor that is being implemented in Iran today and is a part of a new trend that is becoming more and more common as the number of Christian Chinese missionaries increase.

BTJ is a part of a new trend among businesses in Asia where businesses owned and operated as true legitimate businesses are willing to invest and take a risk on mission opportunities, not as a return on a financial investment. Most businesses in places like Indonesia, Philippines, Malaysia, Vietnam, Laos, and Sri Lanka are run by overseas Chinese. These Chinese carry the passports of their current country and often love their homeland very much, but they still feel a strong connection with the land of their ancestors in China. They have heard about the BTJ vision, and they want to support it and be a part of it. They may not understand missions, but they clearly understand the inroads that business can make by building relationships and making a difference for Jesus Christ.

Anyone familiar with the small shopping streets in China will know that the storefront has all the goods but there are bedrooms in the back. The family time, the living space, and the family meals all take place around the business or businesses. Chinese very rarely only have one job. They are entrepreneurs in the real sense of the word and will take many opportunities at the same time.

The Chinese Christians in Iran are not traditional missionaries trained in seminaries and elite Bible schools; they are uneducated farmers and street vendors, and they currently operate in market places around the world already. Their church services back in China often took place in factories, office cubicles, and closed shops. They are not involved in full-time ministry with monthly letters to their donors to give updates about progress. The Back to Jerusalem missionaries have cut their teeth on the hardships of life as they happen on the streets.

BTJ BAM is not a formulated strategy that was conceived in a strategy room of great leaders who congregated together to search for a methodology to effectively proselytize the 10/40 Window. It is merely the best term available to identify what the BTJ missionaries are doing today with business.

The businesses that BTJ currently use in Iran blend in with the environment, which is easy since almost everything in Iran is made in China. The Chinese are not thought of as being evangelists, so this makes them less of a target for the Iranian government.

Another advantage is the small time entrepreneurs from China are also not known for coming to the table with a lot of credit or official bank transfers. Usually, the Chinese show up like they did during the days of the Wild West in America—with their sleeves rolled up, full of hope, and willing to outwork anyone around for less pay than the cheapest laborer.

Setting up a business in Iran has not been easy, but it does provide the support needed for them to adopt Iran as their own country so that they can share the Good News during this dark time in Iranian history.

24

THE FUTURE OF IRAN

I am sitting in a small café in Iran as I write the final chapter of this book. Like much of this book, I will have to smuggle what I write out of the country and pray that I am not caught with it as I walk through security. As I look around the café, I do not see an evil regime wrapped in clergy robes, but instead I see kind faces. I see families walking together. I see young boys wearing Nike shoes and young ladies carrying branded purses. I see a country full of promise.

As I said at the onset of this book, I am not an expert on Iran. I have only been working in Iran for a few short years. This book has been written from the perspective of a Back to Jerusalem Chinese missionary working in Iran.

While I've been writing this book, I have been asked several times what my predictions are for Iran, and each time I have emphatically declined to give any specifics as it pertains to the regime of Iran. The Iranians have to decide their own future.

For many years, Christians have been betting against the Iranian government and predicting the regime will collapse. Articles, books, and studies written by some of the most respected experts in the world have come to the conclusion over and over again that Iran is on the verge of falling apart. There have been many times that the situation in Iran seemed to be at a breaking point, yet today the regime still continues to have absolute control.

Revolutions and regime changes are largely unpredictable. They take a special storm with a unique chain of events and special

185

players. Revolutions that are plotted and financed by secret groups lack the tenacity and passion of real revolutions.

The current leadership in Iran is using fear and oppression against their own people to maintain control, but it must be noted that they have to do this. They no longer have a choice. Their rejection by the people is so widespread that any successful uprising against them would most likely lead to a mass execution of the current leaders.

Things are not good in Iran, and there are several indicators that point to a collapsing regime, but the open secret among the ruling clergy and government leaders is that the current system has to work. Their lives depend on it.

Maybe they have seen video footage of unrepentant tyrants like Romania's former tyrant leader Nicolae Ceausescu who was overthrown by an oppressed people and executed like an animal by a firing squad. Or they've seen the open prosecution of the Gang of Four, those who inflicted so much pain when they carried out Mao Zedong's orders in China.

History tells a story that is not kind to leaders who oppress their own people and lose power.

Iran is currently a country where a revolution can take place anytime. There is popular discontent among the citizens, the economy is in ruins and bankrupt, the ruling circles are aging, and among the younger generation, there are fewer Islamic extremists. The Iranian connection in Iraq, President Al-Maliki, is facing an uprising, the nuclear program is not winning favor with regional powers in the Middle East, and there are reports of severe divisions and internal feuds within the government.

The worse the situation gets for Iran, the tougher they are on their people. With an arrest rate of eighty people per hour and an execution rate of one to two people per day, the Iranian leadership knows that the backlash will not be pretty if the people ever get the upper hand.

Iran's economy shows a 60 percent inflation rate, over 30 percent unemployment, a 300 percent reduction in the value of the national currency, and a negative growth rate. According to Reuters, out of 177 countries rated for the state of their economy, Iran is near the bottom at 168. Only 11 countries in the world have economies worse than Iran.

Iran would like to blame their economic situation on America and the sanctions. In my opinion, economic sanctions never work as a tool to make a tyrannical country change course. If the Iranian economy collapses, it will not be because of the economic sanctions. They didn't work in China or Rhodesia. They didn't work in South Africa during the apartheid. They didn't keep Iraq out of Kuwait. They haven't stopped the blood diamond trade in Africa. They haven't worked for North Korea or Cuba.

In spite of the current sanctions on Iran, their oil exports are actually on the rise. Their biggest customer is China, which has no problem ignoring US complaints. The US has threatened secondary sanctions, or penalties imposed on those who do business with Iran, but China knows that the threats are not effective.

During my short time in Iran, I have learned three things about Iran:

1. Sanctions do not bring about change.
2. The threat of bombing will not bring about change.
3. War (as has been proven in Iraq) is not going to bring about change.

But if there is a prize for the most destructive enemy of the economy in Iran, it is Islam, not the sanctions. The economic woes and domestic poverty in Iran are a result of rigid central planning based on Islam, rather than the sanctions imposed. The only thing that has the power to change Iran is the power of Jesus Christ, and the time is now. Even though Iran is being run by a radical Islamic regime, the people are secular. In fact, Iran may be one of the world's most secular countries, with some reports estimating that mosque attendance is just 2 percent lower than church attendance at the Church of England.

As Back to Jerusalem missionaries continue to work with more and more believers in Iran, we hope for a world that might just have fewer Muslim believers than the number of Communists discovered in Russia after the fall of the Soviet Union.

In other parts of the world, there is a strange phenomenon that shows large majorities desiring the implementation of strict Sharia Law, but the Iranians actually know what that means, and they are not among those who want it.

I might be in the minority, but I no longer believe that a regime change is necessary to bring about a major shift in Iran. I can see that China did not discard Communism and there has yet to be a revolution to change the leadership, but their country has been seeing radical changes economically, politically, and socially, and these shifts are a direct result of revival. China is a better country today because of the radical growth of the church.

What if Iran follows the same path as China? Will a restrictive and dangerous government keep the power of God from moving? Has the control of Communism in China stopped the flames of revival from burning? What if the same God who disappointed the Jewish zealots who were certain that the coming Messiah was going to free them from Roman occupation is the same God who is moving in Iran?

How many Christians will be disappointed when God fails to move in Iran in the way that they feel is necessary? How many will look upon the Christian martyrs in Iran like those who looked upon Christ as He hung on the cross? "And they that passed by railed on Him, wagging their heads, and saying, Ah, though that destroyest the temple, and buildest it in three days, Save thyself, and come down from the cross. Likewise also the chief priests mocking said among themselves with the scribes, He saved others, himself he cannot save. Let Christ the King of Israel descend now from the cross, that we may see and believe" (Mark 15:29–32a KJV).

Watching Christians in Iran persecuted, imprisoned, beaten, and killed feels like a crushing defeat to the church in the way it must have felt when the disciples saw their Lord and King hanging and humiliated on the cross. All of their hopes, dreams, and aspirations were snuffed out as the One they had come to believe in was publicly flogged, humiliated, tortured, and crucified before the entire world.

The idea of a conquering Messiah could not have been more contradictory than the symbol of the cross. The cross was the Roman icon of absolute power. It was a method that communicated the power not only to kill but to kill slowly, methodically, and in the most demonstrative way possible.

Who conquers through defeat? Who brings glory through humiliation? Who claims victory against an enemy who makes a spectacle of the defeated?

The blood of the martyrs in Iran cries out, and like Jesus, their death has brought victory. The persecution and tragic treatment of Iranian Christians since 1979 has brought much sorrow and left a trail soaked in tears, but the redeeming power of love is conquering hearts, even today. Death is not the end for those who believe but is the beginning. And the beginning is not just for those who are martyred, but also for those who are left behind.

Christians around the world rightly pray for the safety of their brothers and sisters in Iran, but what if safety slows the plan that God has prepared for Iran? What if the current tyrannical leadership of Iran is the very factor that makes today's revival possible? History reveals that where there is persecution, Christianity grows.

I will be very honest and say that I really do not want to suffer. I want to avoid it at all cost. In fact, I have invested in many different insurance plans to limit my exposure to suffering.

I also do not want to see others suffer. I really do not want to see families lose loved ones or children see their parents in prison or lose their lives, but as much as I would avoid it, I can't help but be reminded of the sacrificial offering given to me, not only by Christ, but by the founding fathers of every Christian society today: "Father, if thou be willing, remove this cup from me: nevertheless not my will, but thine, be done" (Luke 22:42 KJV). In the midst of the persecution, many, including myself, have received not only salvation but also Bibles in many languages and the freedom of worship. These benefits bestowed on me did not come without sacrifice. They were not a birthright. Someone had to pay the price for my freedoms, and I would be both selfish, self-centered, and, dare I say, not a true representation of Christ's love if I were to believe that my generation should be exempt from paying it forward.

So far, history has taught us that peace for Iran cannot be achieved with violence, bombs, economic sanctions, or even diplomacy. Radicalism in Iran can only be fought and defeated through the radical, sacrificial love of God.

Before America imposes their next economic sanction, they should perhaps sit down with an Iranian missionary and compare the benefit cost ratio of dollars invested. In my opinion, dollar for dollar, the missionary is able to bring about more change than the most highly touted sanction. Before discussions of a bombing campaign are drawn up by NATO forces, it might be worth it to listen to the brave Chinese men and women who are serving in Iran today. At first glance, the mission of the Lord in Iran seems to be full of folly. However, I believe that when the pages of history are finally written for Iran, it will be the unknown Christian soldier who dined at the table of bitter persecution and drank from the cup of sacrifice who pushed back the tides of despair, hopelessness, and abandonment.

If freedom, real freedom, is to be realized in Iran, it will not be through the secular efforts of regime change and economic planning. Real freedom will only be achieved when the Iranians seek the face of God as a nation, for where the Spirit of the Lord is, there is liberty (2 Corinthians 3:17).

What will be more glorious than the day when the Holy Spirit descends upon all of Iran and Jehovah is their God and they become His people?

Notes

Introduction
    1. http://www.thetravelingteam.org/stats.

Chapter 1: A Strategy for Iran
    1. Andrea Palpant Dilley, "The Surprising Discovery About Those Colonialist, Proselytizing Missionaries," *Christianity Today*, January/February 2014, http://www.christianitytoday.com/ct/2014/january-february/world-missionaries-made.html? start=1.
    2. Reza Safa, *The Coming Fall of Islam in Iran: Thousands of Muslims Find Christ in the Midst of Persecution*, Kindle edition, 80.

Chapter 9: The Revolution
    1. *Tahrirolvasyleh*, Volume 2, 494–96.
    2. *Little Green Book,* http://islammonitor.org/uploads/docs/greenbook.pdf, 22.
    3. Ibid., 21.
    4. Ibid., 25.
    5. Ibid., 41.
    6. Ibid., 44.
    7. Ibid.
    8. Ibid.
    9. Ibid., 45.
    10. Ibid.
    11. Ibid.
    12. Ibid., 48.
    13. Ibid.
    14. Ibid., 57.

15. Ibid., 63.
16. http://www.bbc.co.uk/dna/mbreligion/html/
NF2213237?thread=7713263.

Chapter 11: Christian Revival in Iran
1. http://www.muhammadanism.org/farsi/book/
persian_in_bible/persians_in_bible_english.pdf , 78.
2. Ibid.

Chapter 13: Iran's Christian Persecution
1. 2006 country of birth data, Statistics Sweden.

Chapter 14: The Underground House Church
1. Ayatollah Seyyed Ali Khamenei, International
Campaign for Human Rights in Iran 2013 Report, 15,
emphasis added.

Chapter 15: Iran's Secret Army
1. U.S. State Department, Country Reports on
Terrorism 2010, 150.

Chapter 16: The Persecuted of Iran
1. http://www.freefarshid.org.

Chapter 17: A Picture of the House Church
1. *Weekly Evangel*, issue 153.
2. *Weekly Evangel*, issue 154.